Rethinking Cultural Centers

What are cultural centers for? This book offers a unique and dynamic guide to managing these organizations, and the challenge of reconciling cultural aims with business success.

Drawing on research and practice, it provides case-based insights into common managerial problems and their solutions. Although international research demonstrates that culture has positive economic impact and many cultural institutions are multimillion dollar institutions, there has been little research on how cultural centers are managed to combine cultural and economic impact. Due to the diversity of their missions and purpose, cultural centers in Europe often struggle to find business success. By drawing on recent cases from Finland and Sweden, and focusing on the challenges that face both managers and organizations, this book explores the incentives that underpin the foundation of cultural centers, and what is needed to make them a success. By defining the complex challenges that face cultural centers, this book enables managers to move beyond administrating an organization to becoming cultural entrepreneurs, turning good ideas into good business.

In this underresearched area, this book will be essential reading for researchers, policy makers and managers working in cultural centers and museum management.

Tomas Järvinen, DMus, MMus, MSS, Cultural producer, is CEO of Folkhälsan Utbildning Ab, a Vocational Education and Training (VET) school in Finland.

Routledge Focus on the Global Creative Economy
Series Editor: Aleksandar Brkić, *Goldsmiths, University of London, UK*

This innovative Shortform book series aims to provoke and inspire new ways of thinking, new interpretations, emerging research, and insights from different fields. In rethinking the relationship of creative economies and societies beyond the traditional frameworks, the series is intentionally inclusive. Featuring diverse voices from around the world, books in the series bridge scholarship and practice across arts and cultural management, the creative industries and the global creative economy.

Innovation in the Arts
Concepts, Theories, and Practices
Jason C. White

Creative Women in Ireland
Not Your Muse
Aileen O'Driscoll

Cultural Mediation for Museums
Driving Audience Engagement
Edited by Michela Addis, Isabella de Stefano and Valeria Guerrisi

Rethinking Cultural Centers
A Nordic Perspective on Multipurpose Cultural Organizations
Tomas Järvinen

For more information about this series, please visit: www.routledge.com/Routledge-Focus-on-the-Global-Creative-Economy/book-series/RFGCE

Rethinking Cultural Centers

A Nordic Perspective on
Multipurpose Cultural Organizations

Tomas Järvinen

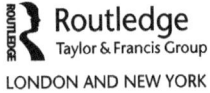

Routledge
Taylor & Francis Group

LONDON AND NEW YORK

First published 2023
by Routledge
4 Park Square, Milton Park, Abingdon, Oxon OX14 4RN

and by Routledge
605 Third Avenue, New York, NY 10158

Routledge is an imprint of the Taylor & Francis Group, an informa business

© 2023 Tomas Järvinen

The right of Tomas Järvinen to be identified as author of this work has been asserted in accordance with sections 77 and 78 of the Copyright, Designs and Patents Act 1988.

British Library Cataloguing-in-Publication Data
A catalogue record for this book is available from the British Library

ISBN: 978-1-032-18210-0 (hbk)
ISBN: 978-1-032-18212-4 (pbk)
ISBN: 978-1-003-25344-0 (ebk)

DOI: 10.4324/9781003253440

Typeset in Times New Roman
by Newgen Publishing UK

Contents

Illustrations

Figures

Tables

Preface

The intention with this book is to offer a unique, dynamic and sharp guide to managing a cultural center. It especially focuses on the new directions in management of such centers as research and practice merge. This book therefore uses cases studies as both a pedagogical tool and an integrating device, focusing on the challenges facing both managers and organizations.

Rethinking Cultural Centers defines the challenges among the cultural centers and enables managers to move from simply administrating an organization to becoming cultural entrepreneurs, where turning good ideas into good business is an everyday routine. It also examines current literature about administration of cultural organization, and offers a rather practical approach to common management issues in the field of (Nordic) cultural centers. By examining six recently (less than ten years ago) founded centers in both Finland and Sweden, this book aims at isolating general strengths and weaknesses, as well as opportunities and treats of cultural centers at large.

While trying to isolate the effects of novel solutions as a result of rethinking the frames for a cultural center, this book is by no means a comprehensive presentation of rethinking cultural centers in the world, Europe, or even Northern Europe. As studies should, it limits itself to a handful of samples and aims at deriving novel thoughts from these. Thus, there are most certainly many apt centers with a high capability of rethinking, and as previous research show us, there are a large number of cultural centers all around the world. The importance of these centers is considerable and is constantly increasing in the local communities where they operate. Interest in these often quite complex institutions is growing rapidly, as is awareness of them among citizens. Due to their versatile mission and societal focus, the cultural centers have had their challenges in finding business success. This book presents the usual incentives to found a Nordic center and what should be focused upon in order to succeed.

This book starts by shortly introducing the evolution of cultural centers in Europe. Due to different backgrounds, the underlying mechanisms for centers differs country wise, and new actors also shape the environments of cultural centers. Although the centers are usually situated within the field business activities, there is a connection to the nonprofit field and thus many centers may be founded on an ideological rather than an economical foundation. This conflict tends to leave many centers in difficult situations. In each chapter this book focuses on common managerial problems and provides case-based insights to solutions.

Rethinking Cultural Centers therefore proposes a revised vision for founding and maintaining cultural centers. As highlighted further on, arts and cultural organizations – where cultural centers are included – do operate under somewhat different principles than solely commercial organization. However, arts and cultural organization that for instance sell tickets or cultural products do come in contact with the commercial market, and would thus benefit from both understanding as well as utilizing tools and knowledge from commercial management of organizations.

Albeit cultural centers are a wide phenomenon throughout the world (over 5000 in Europe alone), the field is very underresearched. Quite surprising, as many of them are multimillion-dollar institutions. The field is also relatively young, which means it is likely to be a growing topic in research. Both the versatility of art forms displayed at these centers, as well the broad economic impact they have on their societies, imply that this is an interesting field for arts managers to study. However, this does not mean that there is not any existing research to draw upon. As an example, one can present the book *Strategic Cultural Center Management*, written by the author of this very book, as well as *Performing Arts Center Management*, edited by Patricia Lambert and Robyn Williams, as well as a handful of interesting articles related to the field.

This book is foremost aimed at managers of cultural centers, although it can also be used by scholars and students, as well as any individuals, private organizations or municipalities that are to found a new cultural center or are already maintaining one (or many!). It is ridiculously easy to get stuck in a mental trap of what a cultural center supposedly should do or how it should be run, when these things vary according to place and needs, as well as over time. In other words, there is always a need to rethink, the cycle never ends. The book will feature examples from the researched cases and relevant quotes that provide real-world examples of principles and theories. Each chapter will also conclude a summary, a balanced assessment of the contribution for cultural organizations and a roadmap for future directions.

It goes without saying that all possible errors and misinterpretations of the informant's statements are the responsibility of the author. The book mainly presents opinions and interpretations by the author, and not those of the informants.

As when writing the aforementioned book on cultural centers, *Strategic Cultural Center Management*, this experience has been somewhat different due to the pandemic and the way it has affected our everyday life. Now we can but hope that the pandemic will not affect the cultural centers anymore, so they can survive and thrive in a postpandemic era – maybe even develop by for instance reading this book!

Acknowledgments

No book is ever written only by the author(s) mentioned on the cover. This book certainly is no exception to the rule. I have many to thank for this final version of *Rethinking Cultural Centers*.

I would like to thank Routledge for the support and for this opportunity – much appreciated! In addition, I would like to thank all the cultural centers that were in the focus of this study; Schaumansalen in Jakobstad (Finland), Kulturhuset Fokus in Karis (Finland), Kvarteret Victoria in Helsinki (Finland), Blivande in Stockholm (Sweden), Komedianten in Varberg (Sweden) and Ifö Center in Bromölla (Sweden). This book would naturally not have been written without your input.

Finally, I wish to thank my family for the inexhaustible support I have received through this journey; my beautiful wife Sofia Eriksson and my lovely children Tilde and Tyra. Without you, nothing really matters.

1 Cultural Centers

A Short Introduction

This book is not intended as a theoretical insight into the world of cultural centers. I will occasionally dwell into some theories, but will mainly have a managerial focus. Why is this? Well, the traditional scientific approach to management declare to provide managers with both the capability to analyze and predict, as well as to control the performance of the complex organizations they lead. But the environment that most managers currently occupy repeatedly seems to be uncertain, unpredictable and even uncontrollable. Science naturally also tackles these areas, but usually through a vast amount of differing theories.

By diving into the everyday life and routines of Nordic cultural centers, this book will hopefully be able to present some focused practical and alternative solutions to the challenges that a cultural center face. In fact, it seems as if no cultural center is ever spared of challenges – which is a good first pointer.

This first chapter will shortly introduce the concept of a cultural center at large, the Nordic cultural centers, the concept of rethinking and a brief overview of the book. Lastly, a summary as well as conclusions.

Chapter Learning Objectives

After reading this chapter, you should know:

- The definition of a cultural center
- How a Nordic cultural center differs from a European center
- What mission focus a cultural center usually has and could have
- The definition of the concept rethinking

DOI: 10.4324/9781003253440-1

1.1 The Culture Center: A Haven for Arts?

First of all, and the question on everybody's lips – what is a cultural center? It will most probably help the common reader to understand the object of this study as well as the manager of such a center to relate to the entire field, if we would start by describing the typical cultural center in Europe. As pointed out in earlier studies (Järvinen, 2021), it may seem obvious at first, but it is not as clear as one may think. Were we to trust Oxford English Dictionary alone, the definition could be the following:

> *A public building or site for the exhibition or promotion of arts and culture, especially of a particular region or people.*
> (Oxford English Dictionary, 2022)

Although Oxford English Dictionary has managed to grasp the essence in one sentence very well, these multifunctional buildings usually differ somewhat internally. In fact, both the size, type and house vary hugely in Europe (Fitzgerald, 2008). Furthermore, a typical feature of the cultural centers is the focus on multiple art forms (Järvinen, 2021).

There are thousands of cultural centers in Europe – the European Network of Cultural Centres, ENCC, represent over 5000 centers in 27 countries alone (ENCC, 2021). These centers combined have several million yearly visitors and yet we know very little about how they engage citizens and of their impact on society (Eriksson et al., 2017). The earlier mentioned lack of research on the cultural centers is due to many reasons, but can to a certain extent be explained by the variety and divergences of the cultural centers. There are numerous forms of centers across Europe and there is not even a consensual name – some call them houses of culture, centers for socio-culture, citizen houses, activity centers and so on.

A cultural center is often defined as a space initiated with the goal of functioning as a means for the distribution of different artistic, cultural, educational, philosophical expressions (Eriksson et al., 2017; Järvinen, 2021). The center is open for everybody in the community with the intention of highlighting and promoting cultural values and activities within the area of its community. A cultural center develops both cultural services and creation and is multidisciplinary to its nature, practice and performing activities, in addition to supporting other cultural organizations. A center usually revolves around a basic space or spaces for presenting cultural services, other rooms for workshops, meetings, exhibitions, libraries and administration offices. Furthermore, a center commonly has a load of bathrooms, restrooms and wardrobes.

Besides performing as a venue for culture, the centers have traditionally integrated a mixture of different aims (Eriksson et al., 2017). These aims combine supporting active citizenship by way of artistic and cultural activities, invigorating deserted industrial buildings and remodeling ignored urban areas, elaborating creativity, society, innovation and entrepreneurship. An ordinary cultural center therefore integrates art and creative activities (with their spaces and technical equipment's for rehearsals, performances, meetings, exhibitions and workshops) by aiming attention on diversity (a multitude of activities, customers and users), community engagement, voluntary workers and receptiveness to initiatives from the grassroots level. As described above, the centers are usually closely linked to the local neighborhood, managing on a comparatively low budget (consisting of public and private funding as well as ticket revenues), providing both open and adaptable spaces and connecting professionals and amateurs along with cultural and collective activities. This becomes apparent in the vision statement of the cultural center Kulturfabrik in Luxembourg (Fitzgerald, 2008, p. 6):

> *To contribute to the cultural and artistic development of the region; to get young people involved in artistic creation and to favor the respect, the understanding and the acceptance of the "other", the "different" and the "strange(r)".*

In addition to painting a picture of what a cultural center is, it is equally as effective to define what it is not; a cultural center is not a building or an organization focusing solely on one artistic discipline – for example, a theater is not a cultural center (assuming it only does theater, that is) (Järvinen, 2021). Furthermore, and as this book will advocate, a cultural center (also) operates within the boundaries of market economy and can thus make good use of tools linked to this field. Still, a cultural center is not to be confused as merely a commercial actor, as it is so much more. It works within the framework of arts and culture, and has as such other goals than making profit. But we will come to this at a later stage.

Trans Europe Halles, a network consisting of 135 cultural organizations from altogether 39 European countries (Trans European Halles, 2022), conducted a survey and a questionnaire where the results implied that average nongovernmental arts/cultural center has a building of about 2500 m² situated in an urban area, with around 200 performing arts or other public events yearly in eight different art forms, and a yearly audience of 75,000. They arrange 50% of their total cultural content, attract more revenues from renting the venues than any other income source, have a staff of 19 and a budget of about 1.25 million euros and a café or bar that usually contributes more to the funding of the center than public funding (Bogen, 2018).

But where should the cultural center be positioned, are they mainly a leisure business? According to Tobelem (2018), they are much more than so – even if they Oalso represent leisure time businesses. The cultural sites – where we easily can include cultural centers – affect positively the development of a region's attractiveness for tourists and serve as a symbol of a city's rebirth. In fact, arts and cultural organizations, the cultural sector and industries account for roughly 2.6% of the complete European GDP (European Commission, 2010).

National and local cultural policies play an extensive role in making cultural spaces (especially the public centers) that promote the urban transformation of a city (Miles and Paddison, 2005; Pratt, 2005). In the wake of this, the necessity to fund cultural spaces mainly for artistic and cultural productions is usually emphasized by the need to support cultural centers that in turn support cultural tourism. This means that the cultural policies need to balance the aims of both tourism and cultural production (Crane, 2002). The cultural centers within a specific region can be considered as a regional arts and cultural industry (or creative sector), both developing and selling cultural products in the shape of events and tangible art.

The cultural tourism set aside, the symbolic value of culture is seen by the cultural policies as critical to the development of the individual. Foucault (1980) saw this as an elementary issue in the process of social management of people. During (1999) in turn observes that cultural policies may shape submissive citizens, whilst Miller and Yudice (2002) notices the development of cultural citizenship and lastly Bennett (1995) thinks cultural policies lessens the differentiation of society by remodeling its citizens into more refined and culturally aware. This could furthermore be developed by adding UNESCO's definition to the concept of cultural services:

> *Services aimed at satisfying cultural interests or needs. They do not represent cultural material goods in themselves but facilitate their production and distribution. For example, cultural services include licensing activities and other copyright-related services, audio-visual distribution activities, promotion of performing arts and cultural events, as well as cultural information services.*
>
> (UIS, 2009)

Jurėnienė (2012) has pointed out that having active cultural centers is a way to secure the decentralization of culture, something that is also promoted by the EU, as well as of national and regional cultural development policy programs. The cultural centers can therefore be under policy agendas as in carefully planned top-down municipal initiatives (Silvanto et al., 2008), but they can just as easily be bottom-up private initiatives of local individuals and/or artists (Informant O). Still, it is of value to examine the political mechanisms behind the development of municipal centers.

In earlier years, the function of culture in policy dialogues was mainly to guarantee the distribution and acknowledgement of culture beneficial to the general public (Mitchell, 2003). In the second half of the 1980s the public funding for both arts and culture were either kept untouched or increasing in Europe. In addition, the structural reform taking place simultaneously, where the decision-making authority was shifted from the central government to either regional or local level, marked an upcoming era of decentralization. Now, this did not go along as easily as one might imagine, it rather ended up in – besides the change in the decision-making structures as well as actors – conflicts and additional types of power concentrations. Besides using arts and culture as something beneficial to the general public, the 1980s also presented an idea of making use of them as an engine for economic growth. In fact, the economic growth philosophy became an elemental part of the cultural policy dialogue in both the EU as in its member states during 1990s. And as a result of the structural reform, also on the regional and local level.

In recent past, there has been an extension of the urban cultural dialogue, namely *the creative city* (Landry, 2000; Florida, 2012). Especially with the triumph of Richard Florida's (2012) account of *the rise of the creative class*, the recognition as to the process of combining creativity and culture in urban policies in favor of attracting more of the so-called creative class has increased. According to Florida (2012), cities will have to and should compete with each other in pursuance of appealing to the creative class both for its economic growth as well as for the cultural vitality. Correspondingly, a contribution to the cultural infrastructure becomes ever more important, which in turn crystallizes the notion of urban cultural strategies. Here we have the cultural center as a somewhat easy answer regarding the dissemination and acknowledgement of culture. Both the location of the cultural center as well as its role as a place for all residents to experience the arts positions it in relation to the city at hand (Peterson, 2002). This indicates that the geographic area of the city where the center is located in and its surrounding suburbs are in many ways defined by the performances in the cultural centers, and the other way around.

However, it is worth noting as well that Florida's (2012) creative cities and creative class has been criticized as well. The disregard of the social position and class consciousness in the concept of creative class could lessen the generalization of its values on its members and thereby cause inequality (Krätke, 2010; Pavelea, 2021). In addition, this inequality amidst the noncreative and creative classes is difficult to diminish as a result of the structural relationship between works and capitalists. Furthermore, the creative economy complies to globalization and by that to the downturn of the traditional manufacturing industry and will as such have an impact on economic growth. As to the aforementioned pandemic, such changes will affect globalization and the mobility of creative ideas and thereby pose a danger to cities.

But although Florida's approach can be criticized for its very supportive concept of class, sociocultural qualities such as cultural life, social and cultural diversity, as well as openness and tolerance do represent significant factors in cities' ability to be attractive and boost their economy (Krätke, 2010).

The features of the field of cultural centers presented above show that different centers can be difficult to compare, and this may as mentioned also have contributed to the shortage of knowledge on the field (Eriksson et al., 2017). At the same time, this may be a characteristic that make the centers especially well-suited for a specific task: as citizen participation usually is refined from the general mission of all these differing centers, they can become (or have already become) influential arenas for daily cultural, democratic and social citizen participation. Regarding this task, the diverseness of economy, organization, size and venue play a secondary role, as the main aim is to include citizens in the sociocultural activities taking place within the cultural centers.

As stated many times above, the field of cultural centers is very underresearched (Järvinen, 2021). Since culture centers can furthermore not be compared with museums more than with theaters or with concert halls since they simply work according to different logics, we cannot make use of merely such studies. There is therefore a need for further academic and managerial studies on cultural centers in order to be able to examine their operating conditions and the organizational field of which they are a part of. This book is an attempt to do just that. Readers wishing to go deeper into the background and definition of cultural centers are advised to consult the works of Fitzgerald (2008), Eriksson et al. (2017) and Järvinen (2021).

1.2 A Brief Definition of Nordic Cultural Centers

The difference between cultural centers in the Nordic countries and rest of Europe (or the world for that matter) is naturally not substantial. But there are differences. And just why would we look into this? Well, firstly because this book uses only Nordic cultural centers as a focus group, and secondly, because it is useful for all the (hopefully) non-Nordic readers to grasp why some things further on in the book may seem odd or so to speak out of tune. So, let's briefly discuss Nordic cultural centers.

According to a study made in 2016, the cultural centers in the North have the highest amount of public funding in Europe (Schiuma et al., 2016). Where southern European centers receive a public funding up to 70% of the total turnover, this report claims that northern centers receive 100%. A tenth of all the centers in the study receive no public funding at all. Now, these figures should be taken with a grain of salt, other studies show very clearly that northern centers do not receive all the needed funding from public authorities (Järvinen, 2021). Still, the study is most probably accurate in displaying a difference in the distribution in public funding between southern and northern European centers, as the northern centers most likely receive more public funding. According to the same study, the average number of annual events in northern centers is 273, in comparison to 295 in western Europe and 105 in both eastern and southern Europe (Schiuma et al., 2016). The northern centers have 166,000 annual visitors, western European centers in turn 114,000, eastern centers 24,000 and southern 14,000.

In an earlier work of Finnish cultural center, a distinction between the types of the existing cultural centers were made, according to ownership and control (Järvinen, 2021). The chances are that the same division can be found elsewhere, but let us still explore the Nordic model. The types found amongst the northern centers are (1) the public centers (maintained by municipalities or the state), (2) the private centers (both private and civil sector, that is, centers maintained by for instance NGO's, foundations, firms or joint stock companies), (3) the hybrid centers (maintained by both private actors as well as the municipality or the state) and (4) the centers maintained by governmental or municipal companies. The idea of this book is not to focus on a specific group of centers, neither is it to extensively juxtapose these groups internally. Still, in order to understand the characteristics between different cultural centers, it is important to be familiar with the mechanics steering each center. Thus, public cultural centers (the most common type in Finland) are usually subject to local cultural services and are therefore funded by the municipalities. The private centers may partly be financed by municipalities, but usually to a much lower degree, and are as a result able in a higher degree to make own decision regarding what to do next. Here both the private and civil sector centers seem to work mostly the same, this is why they are both under the same umbrella of "private centers". The hybrid centers, in Finland at least the smallest as well as the newest group, are a joint venture type, were for instance the maintainer of the services may be a private actor, and the owner of the building the municipality. Here the amount of freedom to make own decisions and thereby financing varies. The centers maintained by governmental or municipal companies are simply an attempt to get more private money in the center by partly privatizing it. According to studies in Finland, this has not quite happened in a desired way (Kangas and Pirnes, 2015).

The informants – which will be more thoroughly introduced in Section 1.4 (but consist of 17 representatives from 3 Swedish and 3 Finnish cultural centers) – were asked to describe their view on culture centers to define the concept. Namely because it may affect the result if the view of this concept differs much between them. The vast majority still defined culture centers in a fairly similar way as in this study. This became clear when an informant described a culture center as: *a versatile house with life and movement, where there is a low threshold to enter. On our part it* [the center] *is for all the inhabitants of the municipality* (Informant F).

Furthermore, the public good in the business of a center was emphasized, because the focus of the mission is, after all, too broad to be described purely as business (Informant L). The focus is also on easy accessibility for outside customers to rent in the venue. A culture center should be available for a nonprofit activity, external attenders should have the opportunity to enter and participate, perhaps rent the venues, the centers should create own cultural content based on own cultural strategies but also on reacting on the environment, strive to include both the professional as well as the amateur field (Informant G).

While many of the descriptions offered by the informants were in line with the general view of cultural centers presented in the preceding chapter, some interpretations arose worth highlighting due to the nuance difference they entail. Firstly, some informants questioned the role of the culture center defining the activity, and above all that if it is the activity that defines the walls:

> *Every physical environment where culture is practiced can be called a culture center. I might say that it is a place where more than just*

a strand of culture is practiced. The physical environment brings together more than just one actor, I would say that makes a cultural property a cultural center in a broader sense.

(Informant B)

Still, the assertion that a cultural center should be open for anyone to rent is something that a few informants of this study problematize, in that the center loses its focus if the quality is too diverse and in such cases the audience may have difficulty understanding the cultural offering altogether (Informant A; Informant O). The belief is that if a center is there not only for professionals, but for culture to exist and be experienced on a broad basis, it may become of a very variable quality and origin. Thus, the cultural center will be lacking an actual concept, and thereby a profile. It is indeed a center for culture, but the audience may have a bit of a hard time knowing what to find there. So, is the cultural center concept in itself a flawed concept? Or should it simply be regarded as a Nordic feature to focus the cultural content of the center? According to Bogen (2018) these differences can be perceived in European centers as well.

Something that has not been emphasized in previous studies of cultural centers is the connection to the external cultural field in addition to what happens in the building itself. Something all the six cases in this study show examples of, is that cultural centers can be a platform for other organizations (or actors) – in the form of, for example, office or working space. It enables a more durable rental income and collaborations between the players.

we gladly want to have cultural producers here, that is, preferably a theater, a music institute, someone who produces art and culture, preferably a gallery. At the same time, we also want to offer space for the civic organizations' administration, e.g. office space for such organizations that work with Finnish-Swedish issues in the culture and education industry.

(Informant E)

The difference here being the duration of the rental contract, that is, instead of all the tenants being short-termed customers with one or a few days on the stage, they rather have other spaces rented for both office functions as well as rehearsal studios and such, on a long-term basis. This gives the cultural center both an economic stability in the shape of steady monthly rental income and easy access to collaborations and daily information about the cultural field itself.

A reinterpretation of the concept of a culture center that most informants contributed with is the interconnecting task that they have in regard to the organizational side. In addition to the classic external tenants that rent the stage (and/or any other spaces) one or many days, the centers in focus of this study show evidence of longer-term thinking in regards to a sustainable economy, with permanent tenants who in addition to their long-term spaces in the centers also can rent the stage from time to time and also otherwise interact with others in the building. These organizations can be everything from smaller theater groups to literary organization, the main thing is to attract organizations (or single artists for that matter) that enhance the variability, strength and collaboration within the cultural center. This gives the culture centers a new dimension in relation to the collaborations and new projects taking form under their roof, as well as a financial security.

1.3 Rethinking as a Concept

The word *rethink* should be familiar to most of us, and would we consult the Oxford English Dictionary (2022), the definition would be *A reassessment, especially one that results in changes being made.*

The current view on strategical management include a rethinking of the practice of leadership as to both practice, style and thinking. There is always a need for managers able to think strategically in this continuously changing world (Ashammari and Akhras, 2017). Transforming the organization is naturally the foundation of any business change (Nadler et al., 1995). This includes rethinking an organization's business practices, operations and structure of the organization in order for it to perform better. The process of rethinking and thereby transforming the organization is both an unending and evolutionary process with the employee in the middle, making him or her the very key element of success.

Shifting consumer habits, technological innovations as well as business model changes (see Section 2.2) are to an ever-greater extent generating instability in organizations. In order to favorably respond to these fluctuations, arts managers need not only be innovative problem-solvers, but also favor predetermined alternatives instead of the traditional decision-making attitude, and thus adopt a design–creating attitude, a rethinking of sorts, by for instance molding new options altogether (Schumacher and Mayer, 2018). As today, this accelerating market shift vis-à-vis integrated services and products has prompted considerable changes to organizational investment in innovation and how they engage with their customers and train their employees.

Rethinking can be seen as an opportunity for your cultural center to advance efficiency, effectiveness and sustainability, both regarding to the internal and external impact. But how do we rethink our cultural center and enable methods such as strategic thinking, transparency as well as optionality without simultaneously losing purpose? Do not worry. This book will get to this further on.

1.4 An Overview of this Book

This book is not designed to dwell extensively in matters closely related to general theoretical approaches, as it aims at presenting a short pragmatic view on administrating cultural centers. Nevertheless, every study can benefit from presenting some basics as to how the study was conducted – otherwise the reader will not have the possibility to assess the trustworthiness of the results. Therefore, a short presentation of the methodology.

1.4.1 Methodology

This study has been carried out as a case study with six culture centers in focus. To achieve the goal of this study, two to four people from each culture center were interviewed, with a total of 17 interviews (9 women and 8 men). The six cases that are in focus are three Finnish; Schaumansalen in Jakobstad, Kulturhuset Fokus in Karis and Victoria kvarteret in Helsinki, as well as the following three in Sweden; Blivande in Stockholm, Ifö Center in Bromölla and Komedianten in Varberg. As will be clear in this section when examining each cultural center more closely, five of the six cases represent private cultural centers. Each center still has quite the different background as well as organizational structure, which makes the combination of cases interesting and in no means a unilateral approach to the concept of a cultural center in general.

When the informants were selected for the interviews, there were certain criteria for the selection. One of these was that the informants needed to be able to contribute with their experiences and experiences of being employed and working for the culture center. There was no particular desire to examine or compare certain occupational groups, the low-skilled with the highly-educated, or men's experiences with those of women. The goal was instead to select informants who represented a diversity of occupations, positions, ages and both men and women. When deciding who to interview, one intention was to go beyond a purely manager focused viewpoint, another to submit all interview data to critical interpretation and avoiding oversimplification by directing too much attention on specific theories. The analysis applied to the collected material is thematic.

The interviewees are fairly evenly distributed across the six culture centers. It is worth noting that the ownership structure affected the need for fewer or more informants, as well as that Kulturhuset Fokus does not yet have an active organizational structure as the others do (the center is not built yet!). The selection also includes several positions such as foundation chairman, producer, administrative manager, construction manager and more. The informants' year of birth was distributed fairly evenly between the 1950s and 1980s. All informants are anonymized in the results of the study and have been assigned a letter between A and Q.

Interviews were chosen as a method for collecting qualitative data, as the format enables a significant study as a two-way communication that provides in-depth descriptions of the topics in this study. Interviews make it possible to collect rich data from people in different roles and situations (Myers, 2009).

In order to avoid missing the informants' own approaches, the interview protocol was not designed around any specific theory or terminology. In this way, their experiences were not colored by any preconceived notions (Gioia et al., 2013). During the interviews, I sometimes briefed the questions and let them follow the questions that came up during the conversation.

1.4.2 The Cases in Focus

Schaumansalen in Jakobstad, Finland. Schaumansalen (the Schauman hall) is located in Campus Allegro in Jakobstad, a campus with spaces for education, library, restaurant and café, bank, shops and offices (Campus Allegro, 2021). Schaumansalen is located in the middle of the Campus and has a variable acoustics, which means that the hall can be used for many different purposes (Schaumanhall.fi, 2021). The concert hall can accommodate just over 400 people, depending on the level at which the orchestra stage is located.

The activities in the cultural center – or mainly the concert hall – is maintained by the limited company Jakobstads Konsertsal Ab, which as the hall itself is owned by Ab Yrkeshögskolan vid Åbo Akademi, which is commonly known as the University of Applied Sciences, Yrkeshögskolan Novia (YH Novia) (Informant J). Campus Allegro, the entirety where Schaumasalen can be found, is mainly owned by the foundation Stiftelsen för Åbo Akademi. This cultural center is more thoroughly introduced as a case presentation in Section 2.5.

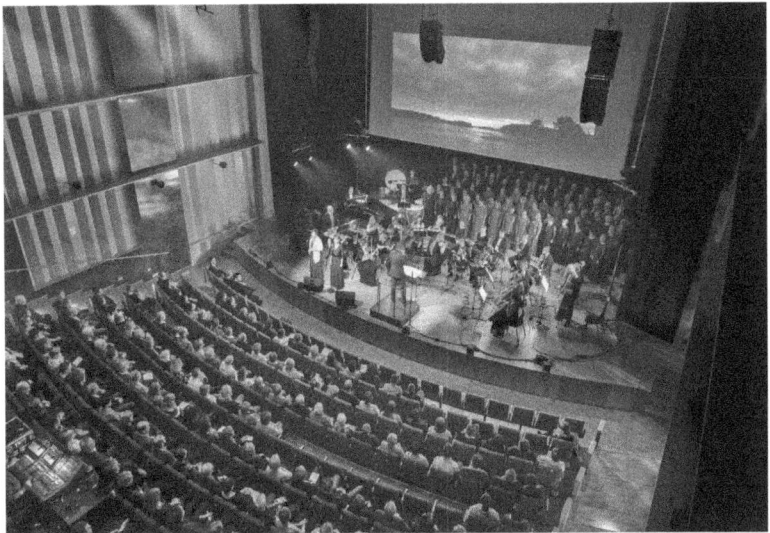

Figure 1.1 The stage of the cultural center Schaumansalen in Jakobstad, Finland. A photograph by Santeri Jutila.

Victoria kvarteret in Helsinki, Finland. Victoria kvarteret (the Victoria district) describes itself as Busholmen's (an area in Helsinki) center for art and culture (Kvarteretvictoria.fi, 2021). The district has a versatile housing for young people, the elderly, families with children, students and artists. In addition, they offer service in the form of culture, a restaurant, offices and day care. Teater Viirus theater acts as the maintainer of the cultural activities in Victoria kvarteret and in addition, many Finnish-Swedish organizations have their offices in the main building for cultural activities.

The cultural venue as well as the organizational center of Victoria kvarteret is owned by Stiftelsen Kvarteret Victoria (Informant B). They also maintain an NGO that manages some of the activities in the center. This cultural center is more thoroughly introduced as a case presentation in Section 4.4.

Kulturhuset Fokus in Karis, Finland. The old cultural venue called the Focus House in Karis was demolished in the spring of 2021 (Svenska Yle, 2020). The construction of Kulturhuset Fokus is planned to be completed in the summer of 2022. The new culture center is

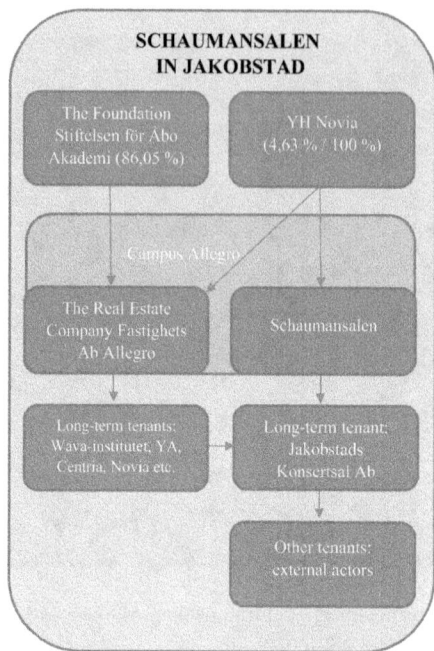

Figure 1.2 The organizational structure of Schaumansalen in Jakobstad, Finland.

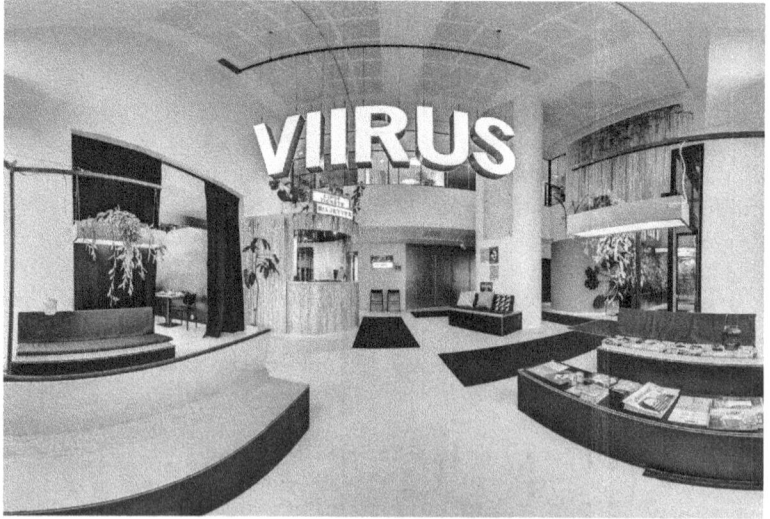

Figure 1.3 The entrance of the cultural center Kvarteret Victoria in Helsinki, Finland. A photograph by Lauri Lundahl.

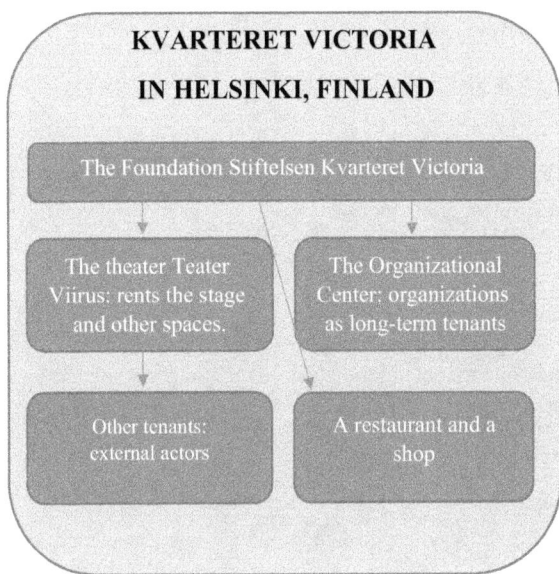

Figure 1.4 The organizational structure of Kvarteret Victoria in Helsinki, Finland.

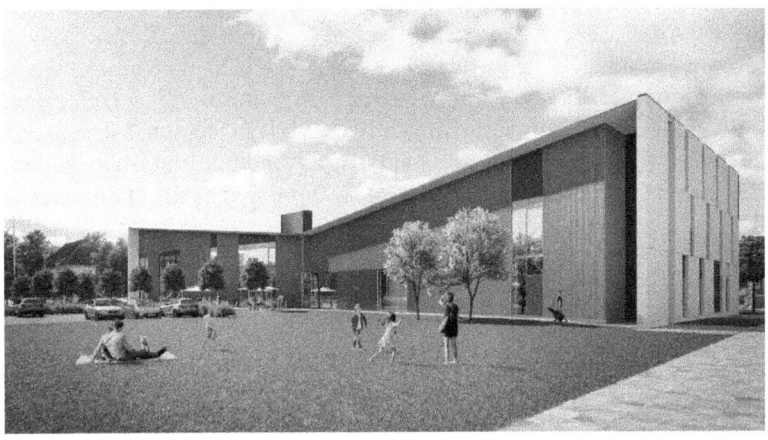

Figure 1.5 The front of the cultural center Kulturhuset Fokus in Karis, Finland. A photograph by Ahlman Arkkitehdit Arkitekter Oy Ab/ Tietoa Finland Oy.

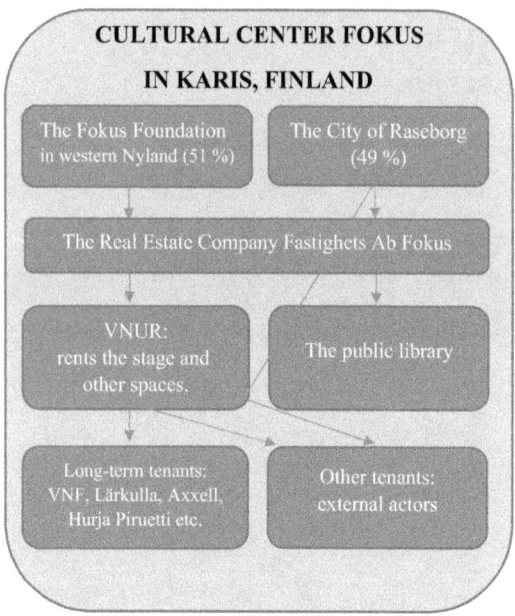

Figure 1.6 The organizational structure of Fokus in Karis, Finland.

administered by a real estate company founded for the purpose, and the city of Raseborg (49%) and the Fokus Stiftelsen i Västra Nyland (Fokus Foundation in western Uusimaa) (51%) – the future owners and maintainers of the cultural center – own the company (Informant C). Västnyländska Ungdomsringen rf (VNUR), a regional service and interest association for youth, local history and cultural organizations in western Uusimaa (Vnur.org, 2021), is appointed as the maintainer of the coming activities in the cultural center.

Blivande in Stockholm, Sweden. Blivande is according to their own definition a place for participatory culture and organizations at Frihamnen, Stockholm, Sweden (Blivande, 2021). According to themselves, they have no single vision. The cultural content is co-created by different people as well as organizations involved. They define the co-creating by citizen initiative as a work of art in itself and a test in creativity and self-organization. Blivande has a container village on their parking lot, with slots for external actors to rent for art and culture, and in their building workshops for craftspeople and creative businesses. This

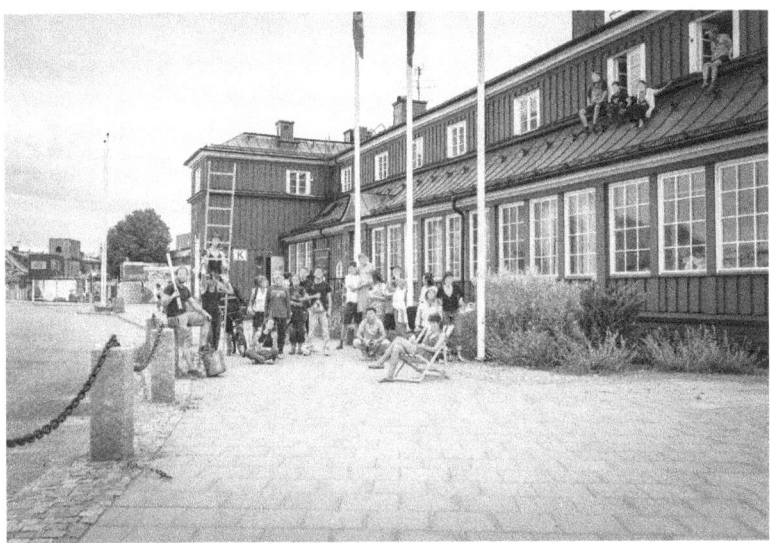

Figure 1.7 The front of the cultural center Blivande in Stockholm, Sweden.
A photograph by KeRer Raudmets.

cultural center is more thoroughly introduced as a case presentation in Section 3.5.

Ifö Center in Bromölla, Sweden. Ifö Center is an artist-run cultural center at Lake Ivö in Bromölla, Sweden (Ifö Center, 2021). The center has a total of 43,000 m² in an old ceramics factory and has opened up the previously closed industrial area of the factory for culture and tourism. Their collective builds everything itself and arranges courses, workshops as well as guided tours. A world-class outdoor gallery is expanding on the factory outer walls, with works by internationally renowned street artists.

Ifö Center is run by the NGO Ifö Center Sambandscentralen, founded in 2014 (Informant O). To create a separate board for the art-hall a second NGO called Ifö Center Exhibit was founded in 2016. Ifö Center Exhibits board works only with exhibition programming, while all other activities as well as the overall coordination and additional help with exhibitions is done by Sambandscentralen. In 2019 a non-profit limited company, Ifö Center Development AB was founded for buying the factory buildings with loaned capital. The nonprofit association Ifö Center Sambandscentralen retains majority ownership in the

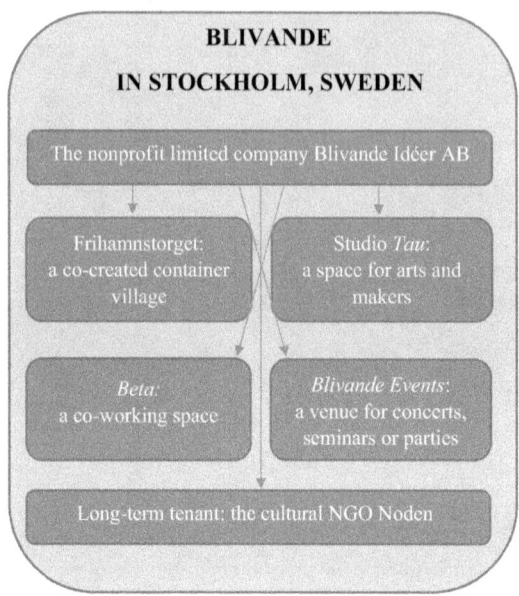

Figure 1.8 The organizational structure of Blivande in Stockholm, Sweden.

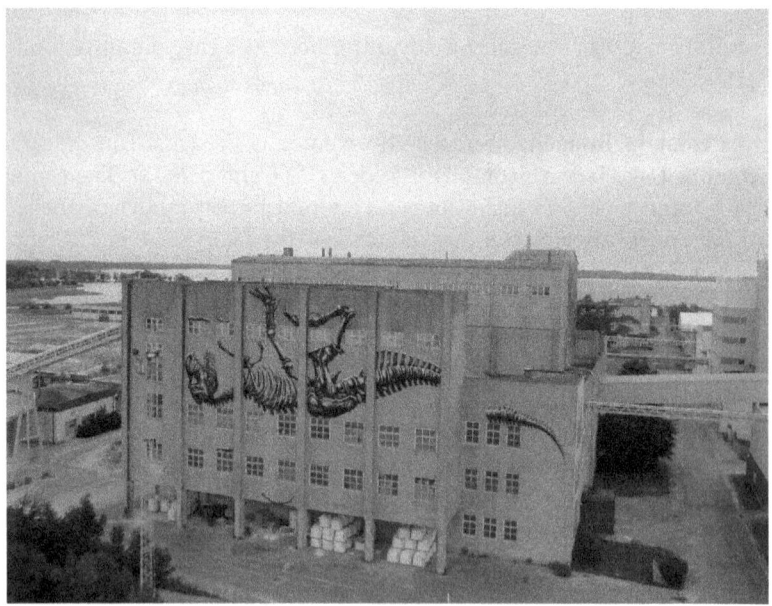

Figure 1.9 The front of the cultural center Ifö Center in Bromölla, Sweden. A photograph by Ifö Center, Ifö Center Outdoor Gallery, painting by ROA.

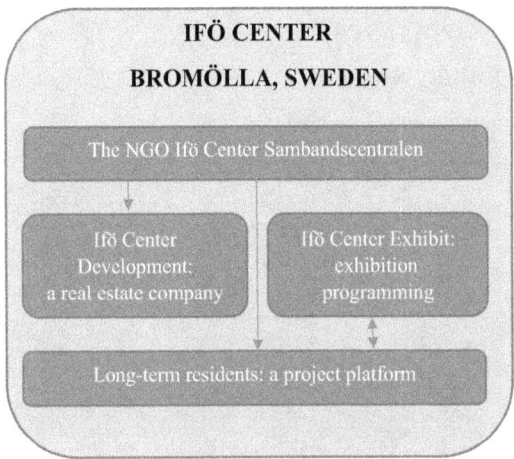

Figure 1.10 The organizational structure of Ifö Center in Bromölla, Sweden. A photograph by Varbergs kommun.

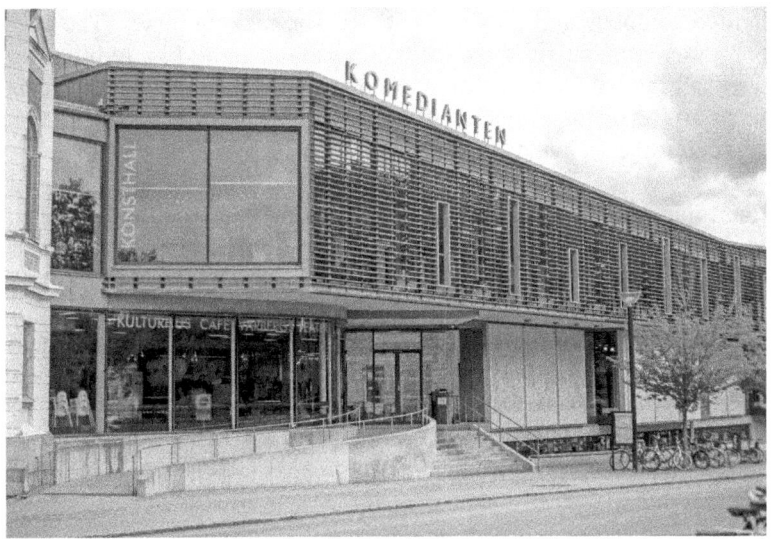

Figure 1.11 The front of the cultural center Komedianten in Varberg, Sweden.

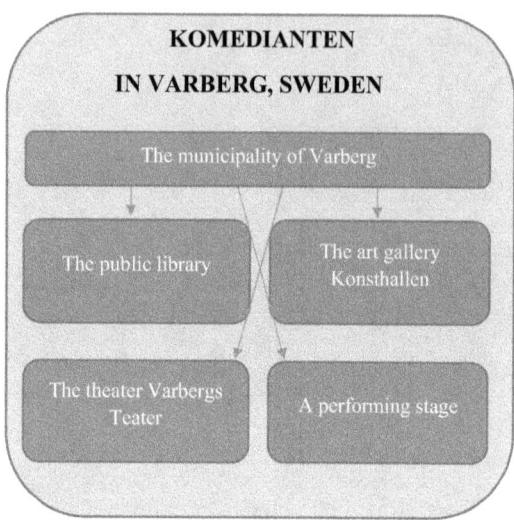

Figure 1.12 The organizational structure of Komedianten in Varberg, Sweden.

limited company and thus has sole decision-making power. The company was founded via a crowdfunding campaign and in addition has over 550 shareholders who all pitched in to help buy the buildings. The sole purpose of the company is to secure the spaces and support for art and cultural activities at Iföverken.

Komedianten in Varberg, Sweden. Komedianten is a cultural center in Varberg, Sweden. This cultural center has a public library, art gallery as well as a performing stage (Informant M; Informant N). The library, which is the main public library in Varberg municipality, has been at this location since 1981. During 2010–2012, the library was expanded with an additional floor and converted to the current arts center, which was opened on 14 January 2012. The theater has been there since 1895 but is not integrated in the cultural center. The name of the cultural center comes from the theater. Komedianten is a public cultural center, that is, a center maintained by the municipality.

1.5 Summary and Conclusions

Before moving on to the following chapters, this first chapter needs a summary and some conclusions. One reason for not focusing solely on theories in this study was due to the aim of open-mindedly examining the Nordic cultural centers if there could be found general solutions adaptable for centers elsewhere. While looking through the lenses of a specific theory, the tendency is to search for specific answers to specific questions. This study strives to disregard such a restricted view in favor of a more tolerant exploration.

Every cultural center has their own unparalleled characteristics, their own unique background, stakeholder networks, opportunities, threats, strengths and weaknesses – as well as markets that function according to different dynamics. Ergo, every cultural center needs to pave their own way. But it is important that they do so in an informed way. That is where this book comes in to the picture. It is not so much about the Nordic cultural centers differing from their European peers, it is rather that every single cultural center tends to have specific features that is a result of the requirements of that specific region. Therefore, it should be worthwhile to generalize the results of studying only Northern centers.

The informants believe that culture centers are a place open for everyone. Diverse cultural activities for all kinds of practitioners and the general public are conducted in the centers. The informants supplement the traditional definition of cultural centers by adding the permanent tenants in the form of organizations or other cultural entrepreneurs that both collaborate, develop the business and contribute to a more stable economy for the center. Some of the informants emphasize the need to rethink this very general mission statement by adding the need to focus on some specific cultural areas in order to maintain high quality in the cultural offering as well as meeting the customers' requirements. This too may be seen as a regional feature, as the case may be that the region already has for instance a theater or a music hall and there is no point in competing on every possible level. However, it does challenge the common view of a cultural center as "something for everyone" and draws attention to rethinking the general mission statement.

Furthermore, the emphasis on long-term tenants supplies the cultural center with both a dynamic focal point for arts and culture in the region, a steady income and plenty of possibilities for productive collaborations.

Next, we will move on to examine the business approach of cultural centers and their ideological standing. As in arts and culture generally, these two tend to clash, leaving the organization in an either-or situation. But does it really have to be so?

1.6 Practical Recommendations

- Cultural centers differ somewhat internally, but can mainly be seen as a space initiated with the goal of functioning as a means for the distribution of different artistic, cultural, educational, philosophical expressions. The center is open for everybody in the community with the intention of highlighting and promoting cultural values and activities within the area of its community.

- A cultural center should strive to become an answer to the specific cultural shortcomings of the region.
- By collaborating with other complementary organizations, the cultural center may have an advantage both in regards to the cultural offering, beneficial collaborations as well as in the shape of long-term tenants.
- By focusing the mission statement somewhat, the cultural center can productively enhance both the quality of the cultural offering as well as engage more audience.

Application Exercise

Imagine you are planning to found your own cultural center. If you already work at one, you can still do this exercise. Try to define how the cultural center would fit (if already existing; fits) into your specific environment and describe why there is a need for one? A bonus assignment – explain how it could reach (or reaches) a sustainable economy.

References

Ashammari, G., & Akhras, N. (2017). Strategic thinking & its relationship with the big five personality traits among the heads of academic departments at Jouf University. *Journal of Educational & Psychological Sciences*, 18(3), pp. 447–475.

Bennett, T. (1995). *The Birth of the Museum: History, Theory, Politics.* New York: Routledge.

Blivande (2021). *A new world awaits.* Webpage. Accessed: 9.12.2021, available: www.blivande.com/

Bogen, P. (2018). *Stronger Arts and Cultural Organisations for a Greater Social Impact. Business Models Profiling of Cultural Centres & Performing Arts Organisations.* Sweden: Trans Europe Halles, Creative Lenses.

Campus Allegro (2021). *Campus Allegro.* Webpage. Accessed: 26.10.2021, available: https://campusallegro.fi/om-campus-allegro.

Crane, D. (2002). Culture and Globalization: Theoretical Models and Emerging Trends. In: *Global Culture: Media, Arts, Policy and Globalization.* Ed.: Crane, D., Nobuko Kawashima, N., & Kawasaki, K. New York: Routledge, pp. 1–21.

During, S. (1999). *Introduction.* In: *The Cultural Studies Reader.* Ed.: During, S. New York: Routledge, pp. 1–30.

ENCC (2021). *ENCC Network.* Webpage. Accessed: 7.1.2022, available: https://encc.eu/index.php/network

Eriksson, B., Møhring Reestorff, C. & Stage, C. (2017). *RECcORD– Rethinking Cultural Centres in a European Dimension.* Project rapport. Accessed: 31.12.2021, available at: https://encc.eu/sites/default/files/2017-11/reccord_research_final_report.pdf

European Commission (2010). *Green Paper–unlocking the potential of cultural and creative industries.* Accessed: 12.1.2022, available at: https://op.europa.eu/en/publication-detail/-/publication/1cb6f484-074b-4913-87b3-344ccf020eef/language-en

Fitzgerald, S. (2008). *Managing Independent Cultural Centres. A Reference Manual.* Asef, Artfactories and Trans Europe Halles. Accessed: 14.2.2022, available at: www.artfactories.net/IMG/pdf/Managing_Independent_Cultural_Centres.pdf

Florida, R. (2012). *The Rise of the Creative Class Revisited (Tenth Anniversary Edition).* New York: Basic Books.

Foucault, M. (1980). *Power/Knowledge: Selected Interviews and Other Writings, 1972–1977.* Ed. Gordon, C. New York: Pantheon Books.

Gioia, D. A., Corley, K. G., & Hamilton, A. L. (2013). Seeking qualitative rigor in inductive research notes on the Gioia methodology. *Organizational Research Methods,* 16, pp. 15–31.

Ifö Center (2021). *Ifö Center utlyser AIR2–sök ett fritt arbetsstipendium!* Accessed: 21.2.2022, available at: www.ifocenter.com/

Järvinen, T. (2021): *Strategic Cultural Center Management.* New York: Routledge.

Jurėnienė, V. (2012). The role of cultural centres in the fields of children and youth artistic education. *Procedia–Social and Behavioral Sciences,* 51, pp. 501–505.

Kangas, A., & Pirnes, E. (2015). Kulttuuripolitiikan päätöksenteko, lainsäädäntö, hallinto ja rahoitus. In: *Taiteen ja kulttuurin kentät. Perusrakenteet, hallinta ja lainsäädäntö.* Ed.: Heiskanen, I., Kangas, A. & Mitchell, R. Helsinki: Tietosanoma Oy, pp. 23–108.

Krätke, S. (2010). 'Creative cities' and the rise of the dealer class: A critique of Richard Florida's approach to urban theory. *International Journal of Urban and Regional Research,* 34(4), pp. 835–853.

Kvarteretvictoria.fi (2021). *Organisationer.* Webpage. Accessed: 26.10.2021, available at: www.kvarteretvictoria.fi/organisationer

Landry, C. (2000). *The Creative City: A Toolkit for Urban Innovators.* London: Earthscan Publications.

Miles, S., & Paddison, R. (2005). Introduction: The rise and rise of culture-led urban regeneration. *Urban Studies,* 42(5/6), pp. 833–839.

Miller, T., & Yudice, G. (2002). *Cultural Policy.* London; Sage Publication.

Mitchell, R. (2003). Nordic and European Cultural Policies. In: *The Nordic Cultural Model.* Ed.:Duelund, P. Copenhagen: Nordic Cultural Institute, pp. 437–478.

Myers, M. D. (2009). *Qualitative Research in Business and Management*. London, UK: Sage.

Nadler, D., Shaw, R., & Walton, A. (1995). *Discontinuous Change: Leading Organizational Transformation*. San Francisco, CA: Jossey-Bass, Inc. Publishers.

Oxford English Dictionary (2022). *Cultural centre*. Webpage. Accessed: 1.8.2022, available at: www.lexico.com/definition/cultural_centre

Pavelea, A. M., Neamtu, B., Nijkamp, P., & Kourtit, K. (2021). Is the creative class a game changer in cities? A socioeconomic study on Romania. *Sustainability*, 13, p. 5807. https://doi.org/10.3390/su13115807

Peterson, M. (2002). Performing the "People's Palace" musical performance and the production of space at the Chicago Cultural Center. *Space and Culture*, 5(3), pp. 253–264.

Pratt, A. (2005). Cultural industries and cultural policy: An oxymoron. *International Journal of Cultural Policy*, 11(1), pp. 31–44.

Schaumanhall.fi (2021). *Om Schaumansalen*. Webpage. Accessed: 26.10.2021, available: https://schaumanhall.fi/om-schaumansalen.

Schiuma, G., Bogen, P., & Lerro, A. (2016). *Creative Business Models: Insights into Business Models of Cultural Centers in Trans Europe Halles*. Lund, Sweden: Trans Europe Halles.

Schumacher, T., & Mayer, S. (2018). Preparing managers for turbulent contexts: Teaching the principles of design thinking. *Journal of Management Education*, 42(4), pp. 496–523.

Silvanto, S., Linko, M., & Cantell, T. (2008). *From Enlightenment to Experience: Cultural Centers in Helsinki Neighbourhoods*. International Journal of Cultural Policy, 14(2), pp. 165–178.

Svenska Yle (2020). *Byggstarten för nya kulturhuset i Karis skjuts fram–stiftelser och fonder stöder bygget med över fem miljoner*. Webpage. Accessed: 26.10.2021, available: https://svenska.yle.fi/artikel/2020/02/20/byggstarten-for-nya-kult urhuset-i-karis-skjuts-fram-stiftelser-och-fonder-stoder

Tobelem, J.-M. (2018). Are Cultural Sites Leisure Businesses? In: *Culture, Innovation and the Economy*. Ed.: Mickov, B., & Doyle, J.E. New York: Routledge, pp. 84–97.

Trans European Halles (2022). *About us*. Webpage. Accessed: 16.2.2022, available at: https://teh.net/about-us/

UIS (2009). *Cultural services. UNESCO Framework for Cultural Statistics*. Homepage. Accessed: 31.12.2021, available at: http://uis.unesco.org/en/gloss ary-term/cultural-services

Vnur.org (2021). *Västnyländska Ungdomsringen rf (VNUR)*. Webpage. Accessed: 5.11.2021, available at: www.vnur.org/vnur/om_oss

2 The Business Approach and the Core Values

Cultural centers usually tend to be more ideological than pure business organizations; however, a business approach is needed. There is a need for a balance between this approach and the ideological foundation. It should rather be perceived as a natural order and a possibility to further enhance the facilitation of arts and culture by accepting the necessity of an economic awareness.

The focus on profitability can weaken the cultural content production, which in turn can be distorted into a repetitive product without any connection to creative work. However, it can also prove difficult to create profitability if the artistic goals are to be the sole governing mechanism. The same applies to the opposition between arts and buildings.

Using tools such as business models has traditionally not been well received in the cultural sector. The goal of a business model is nevertheless to create a clear and distinct plan for the organization's business operations and a basis for investigating opportunities for future development.

Before we begin our journey into this chapter, we will have to define our route. Or otherwise, it seems (according to the citation above), no road will take us there. A cultural center may have its fingers in many cultural bowls (albeit commonly not in the production of the arts itself), yet there is still a need for both a mission and a strategy. You need to know what you are supposed to do and how you will do it. Otherwise there will not be any road for you to choose, nor a destination. The core values of cultural organizations tend to be more altruistic and not-for-profit than those of pure business organizations, but this does not mean there would not be a need for a business approach – rather there is a need for a balance between this approach and the core values.

By discussing businesses, the focus of this book is as mentioned on the managerial models and processes that are required when producing and exchanging value of the arts and cultural offering taking place in a

DOI: 10.4324/9781003253440-2

cultural center. We are not talking about the arts itself. Nor business in its purest form. Only about the necessity to have a sustainable economy. Still, the balance between arts and economics tend to get blurred or one-sided in many arts and cultural organizations.

It is also worth noticing that the concept of *art economics* has expanded into *cultural economics*, which means that the use of economic reasoning has been expanded from concepts such as *fine-art* and *not-for-profit*, to *the cultural industries* or the *creative industries*, which includes both such actors that operate in the commercial or the for-profit sector. However, this has not gone by without some resistance. For instance, Throsby (2010) has a derogative analysis on the *commodification* of culture and Frey (2003) basically neglects the for-profit sectors in his analysis of cultural policy altogether.

So, is the balance between business and core values of cultural centers a mixture doomed to fail or something possible to maintain? Where should the cultural centers position themselves on the scale between these opposites? The artists presenting their work in cultural centers may give one perspective to the role of the centers – are the cultural centers really supporting arts or just a building? On the other hand, the strictly financial side of administrating a cultural center surely gives the other perspective of the center, that is, the organization needs to have a plan how to make financial ends meet, or there will be no supporting of the arts either.

This chapter will not however mainly focus on the need of strategies, rather it will examine the quintessential contradiction between arts and economics, review the concept of business models, delve into the matter of supporting arts or merely maintaining a building, predicting the future by using current issues as a stepping stone and presenting a case before finishing with a summary and conclusion.

Chapter Learning Objectives

After reading this chapter, you should learn:

- How arts and economics are intertwined
- The scope and advantages of a business model
- The role of the cultural center building
- Current issues that affect the administration of a cultural center and one way to deal with those
- What to consider when organizing a cultural center

2.1 Arts and Economics

Before contrasting arts with economics, it should be concluded that any simple opposition amidst economic and artistic values is challenging to confirm in any organization (Eikhof and Haunschild, 2007), but the tensions are additionally marked in arts and cultural organizations. Still, as both are substantial features of managing a cultural center, this opposition should at least be discussed.

Arts and culture may not be the uppermost necessity to life, nor can they replace other social conditions of life, but they do play a role amongst the basics needs for humans, as in participation, freedom of expression and creative encounters (Zembylas, 2019). Some readers might disagree with this, and consequently it would be good to state that this book is not about disentangling the societal value of arts, rather to honestly place it accurately in relation to life's other necessities. But as a focus on participation, freedom of expression and creative encounters was established, one might at least conclude that arts and culture are not just about generating monetary profit. Although, nor is it only about aesthetics and entertainment – it is also about well-being and public goods. Traditionally the way of thinking has however been that by focusing on the arts and creativity alone, everything else will follow.

It is no overstatement to claim that the debate about which should come first, arts or economics, has become something of a regular feature amongst arts organizations (Järvinen, 2021). This phenomenon goes back to the 19th century and is all about the artistic world not appreciating the economy influencing the creative work (Germain-Thomas, 2019). In traditional market exchanges, it is about satisfying customer needs. But in the sector of culture, this may not always be the case – an artist may aim at challenging or surprising the audience and not clearly satisfy any (traditional) needs (Informant A). Still, as soon as a creative work becomes a part of a business transaction, it goes from being arts alone to the scope of a market. In fact, as Theodor Adorno (1991) highlighted, the customer actually pays in the market for a product when buying a ticket. It is about exchanging value and thus to assess the value of the cultural goods. While the cultural goods in many respects are incomparable to other goods, they still fall into the into the same *whole of commodities that are produced for the market, and are aimed at the market* (p. 38).

So, which side should a cultural center choose? Well, the simple answer would be both. These two different sides of the coin, arts and economics, are fundamentally interlocked. With no real content, not artistic nor value-based, there can naturally not be sufficient revenues and thus a sustainable economy – at least not in the long run. But, naturally the same applies the other way around, that is, without funds to operate, no cultural center can succeed. Furthermore, the line gets blurry nowadays; cultural managers tend to get involved in the creation of arts and culture, whereas artist in turn are included in both management and administration (McCall, 2019). This can be seen as a sign of accepting the duality of the game, but it is no indication that the balance is in place.

Thus, cultural centers should preferably have an insight in economical strategies, the side that usually gets neglected. It is naturally important to cherish and develop the creative work, but without customers paying for the (e.g.) tickets, there will not be any creative work – or at least not a cultural center – whether the artists goal was to meet the customers' needs or to challenge them. But where is the crossroad between arts and economy? When does an organization stress both sides sufficiently? It is said that the more you do for culture, the worse it will turn out (Adorno, 1991). The idea here is to show the paradox of culture; when administrated, it will get damaged. But equally, when left alone, it will lose its effect and quite possible, its existence. Therefore, it can be concluded that the balance between arts and economics does not have a favored formula; each organization has to figure out this individually. The bottom line is however to highlight both sides adequately as an arts manager.

Still, transferring rules or guidelines straight from business management literature is not sensible – it is of importance to understand that cultural organizations differ from other types of business enterprises, if one is to guide the establishment toward success (DeVereaux, 2019). As Tobelem (2018) put it:

> *The stakes are high, for if the cultural institutions must demonstrate their management capabilities and be accountable for their actions to their board or to local authorities, their financial success (which paradoxically could justify the withdrawal of their financers) should nevertheless not allow it to be forgotten that their mission of general interest […] is not profitable and consequently will continue to call upon the intervention of public authorities and/or donors (individuals, foundations, corporations), according to their respective institutional system and legal framework.*

One reason why arts and cultural organization may be strangers to the concept of business, is that they usually dwell in an economic reality not accustomed to making lots of revenues. As one informant of this study put it: [...] *I think we do not have so many contradictions because I think everyone still knows that we make no money to speak of* (Informant K). This lack of money also tends furthermore to result in a heavy reliance on volunteers – which in turn leads to a lack of strategic planning (Bienkowski, 2019). While these volunteers may be able to invest a lot of time into the organization, this investment may still vary quite a bit over time and occasionally leave the organization in quite an unsteady situation. In addition, volunteers in arts organizations come with a heavy package of personal interest in arts and culture, which by no means lightens the heavy weight of arts in favor of economics. Arts managers should consequently keep the staff – be that employees or volunteers – sitting steadily in the boat; a cultural center is, as described above (Section 1.1), not a producer of arts and culture, but merely a facilitator of such. Thus, there is a need for a commercial approach as well.

As organizations that do not produce their own cultural events (Järvinen, 2021), cultural centers mainly deal with customers – both those who produce arts and cultural events, as well as those that attend as audience. Thus, the customer, not the cultural content, lies at the core of the centers value proposition (Addis and Rurale, 2021). A lack of an understanding of the customer leads to a loss of the market as well as the customer base. Therefore, customer experience and customer loyalty should be the main pillars to analyze, define and cultivate for any cultural center. Whatever is to be sold, this will not happen without customer engagement. This is not to say that a cultural center should only focus on satisfying customer needs, but are they to be challenged or surprised (as presented earlier), one needs to know what challenges or surprises them.

Still, this ever-ongoing discrepancy between arts and business does not need to mean an either-or sort of problem, rather this balancing act could be interpreted as a much-needed value indicator of staying true to the organizational values – whilst optimizing the business side to the activities. As Carbonare and Prokupek (2021) pointed out, becoming entrepreneurial does not necessarily imply being commercial or compromising the values of the organization. Operating in a field where there is a thin line between entrepreneurialism and organizational values does limit the organizations options, but only if the organization is willing to limit itself according to current opinions about how an actor within the arts and cultural sector should perform. Being entrepreneurial does, as stated above, not mean abandoning your core values. As one informant in this study emphasized:

> *the purpose of this is not to make money or to enrich me or others who work here. The aim is to create a place where we can create large-scale*

works of art, where we can help different people in different situations, where we can have a meeting place and show art, draw people to the place and so on. It's about opening up opportunities and opening up this room more.

(Informant O)

In order to create that place where large-scale works of art can be created, there needs to be an economic sustainability and a vision as to how it will continue to evolve. In general, many informants wish that culture centers would not be burdened with traditional frameworks for business activities, but at the same time they emphasize the importance of trying to take advantage of different business solutions – even if it would lead to several failures. The important thing is to understand that it takes a long time to build a sustainable business.

You have to dare to fail more, you have to allow failures. Because just by allowing failures, anything can happen. So, you have to have longer-term plans. You cannot build a vision for three years, projects for only three years, and then see what happens, and then they are supposed to continue on their own. There is no such thing. … very few projects are commercially viable after three years.

(Informant C)

It must be emphasized that the point with plans are naturally to avoid failures, but the informant above most likely wanted to highlight the inevitability with plans – *some* may fail even with an abundance of time invested in them. But this should not be let to hinder the arts manager, as *most* plans will fail without sufficient practical input in advance.

Naturally the balance between creative work and commercialism (or simply sound economics) can be examined in a magnitude of angles, not only regarding the, quite frankly, somewhat simplistic discord between arts and economics. As the informant below continues emphasizing – after positioning themselves with sufficient clarity on the well-being side of the debate (that is arts in favor of economics) – there is a political, or should we say social aspect to the matter.

What are we to have art for? Is the point that you should make money from it or is the point that it should further develop us as human beings? That is also why it gets a little bit funny when you call us a private initiative, and that we are in a way, but politically we are very far to the left when it comes to the idea of solidarity.

(Informant O)

As can be seen above, the not-for-profit approach is a strong incentive, and as such, it may color the approach to managing an organization and in worst cases hinder and thus limit the organization. However, the common principles are also the foundation of business and organizational values. But there is not a contradiction between having altruistic core values and managing an organization with *the art of business*. For whatever the values of the organization, there is no virtue in not being effective. One might even say that whatever the aim, the result will have a much wider impact with a carefully applied strategy to get there. Now, this does not mean that an organization playing for the left political division ought to refocus by getting more commercial – in order to then be more uncommercial again with their cultural content so as to stay true to their mission. This does not make any sense, of course. Rather they need to focus on where they can make the money needed for the everyday economy, since the need for money will not diminish even if it is not what this specific organization focuses on within the frames of its mission. It all boils down to efficiency; how to be able to invest the most time and other resources possible in implementing the mission of the organization.

If we can at this point agree on the necessity of both arts and economics, it is probably also fair to say that there is a need of market evaluation and basic research in order for an organization to survive and thrive. If that is the case, there should not either be a problem in having a business model – since a business model really is only about having a strategy for assessing the market, evaluating the successes and failures and predicting the future for the sake of staying ahead of the competition (Falk and Shepard, 2006). Although the more traditional business models are said to prevent the arts organizations from taking any risks and thereby advancing innovations (Carbonare and Prokupek, 2021), a well assembled and applied business model focuses the organizational objectives, by both avoiding unnecessary risks and enhancing innovation. The arts management should strive to react to trends and have open dialogues that may lead to innovation, but still stay focused on the core mission and not be led astray. But let us not get ahead of the game. More about business models in the next section.

2.2 Business Models

The goal of a business model is to create a clear and distinct plan for the organization's business operations and a basis for investigating opportunities for future development (Osterwalder and Pigneur, 2010). The cultural centers should be ambitious enough in their operations to withstand competition. Now, an easy answer would be that cultural centers are not in the business of competing, rather in facilitating arts. But then again, everything that for instance revolves around selling tickets boils down to attracting customers, which in turn translates to competing with anything those customers could choose to do rather than coming to a cultural center. The same applies to tenants. So yes, a cultural center is very much in a competitive market.

The concept of the business model became more popular in the 1990s (Chesbrough, 2011), even if it appeared in the literature already in the 1950s (Drucker, 1954). Today, it can not only be found in the literature, but also in use by especially the business sector (Zott et al., 2011). It should be recognized that the objective of the business model concept has historically been outlined by highlighting value creation as a component of managing the advancement of new emerging technology (Teece, 2010). But there are naturally quite a few different definitions of business models in the academic literature

- A business model illustrates how organizations create, deliver and capture value (Osterwalder and Pigneur, 2010).
- A business model is a conceptual representation of a specific aspect of an organization's strategy; it summarizes the fundamental details you need to know to grasp how an organization can successfully distribute value to its customers (Magretta, 2002).
- A business model is a representation of an organizations fundamental core logic and strategic alternatives for building and capturing value in a value network (Shafer et al., 2005).

Even though there is no distinct or universal definition of the concept of a business model, it seems as if many authors use the definition by Osterwalder and Pigneur (2010). So too will this study, especially as the aforementioned authors emphasize that new business models cannot only be identified in simple monetary terms. This fits neatly with arts and cultural organizations, due to them having many dimensions of value in society, including cultural and social values. In practice, these organizations still need to rethink their business model (since every organization has one whether aware of it or not) on a continuous basis, to better face the challenges a competitive environment poses on them (Carbonare and Prokupek, 2021).

Business model innovation is recognized as a significant component in rethinking the competitive advantage of an organization (Amit and Zott, 2012). A business model is much harder for competitors to duplicate than merely a new product. The components of a business model can be innovated in various ways; content (by adding new activities), governance (by changing who carries out the activities) and structure (by connecting the activities in new ways). Thus, Amid and Zott (2012) propose that business model innovation is the very essence to rethinking process and product innovation as well as the competitive advantage of the organization. By this they mean that every organization has to analyze how they aim to create, capture and thereafter communicate value to their customers – and cultural centers are no exceptions to this.

Using tools such as business model innovation has traditionally not been well received in the cultural sector, mostly due to reluctance toward the concept of *business* (Carbonare and Prokupek, 2021). It has been considered to be a commercialization and thereby in opposite to cultural activities. Nevertheless, this has changed somewhat during the past decade. As the audience is overwhelmed with alternative leisure time entertainment, cultural centers have to rethink their approach and be more entrepreneurial – while still staying true to their values and mission. A professionalization process amongst cultural organization has begun already in the 1960s, which has led for instance to cultural management occupations, publications and special training programs (Mangset, 1995).

Stuba Nikula made a distinction between four models amongst European cultural centers according to the results of a questionnaire in 2016 (Bogen, 2018). There have been some attempts in distinguishing different models before, and as is explained in this attempt, the categorization is rough and leaves quite a few blank spots. Still, it may be of use to take a short closer look at these, as they give an approximate picture of applied models. These models are the (1) *department store*, (2) *the charity shop*, (3) *the shopping mall* and (4) *the boutique*.

The Department Store. A center managed by one organization with various types of products and services to the customers. The center curates most of its cultural content, but does rent out spaces either on a long-term or on a short-term basis. With policies that regulate what types of events can be presented, it assures these to be compatible and aligned with their purpose, mission and values. The Department Store often focuses on one or two main art forms and run the majority of its services such as a bars and cafés.

The Charity Shop. This is a center initially started by for instance occupying or finding a deserted building and initiated scarce finances or resources. The case may also be that they have no paid staff and the work is accomplished by volunteers. Though a formal organizational structure, still informal without official employee roles. Artists and arts organizations frequently donate some services and goods then sold by the Charity Shop.

The Shopping Mall. A decentralized center with no single organization controlling its cultural offering and other activities, rather various organizations and groups that makes decisions about this – with a very diverse and varied output. The governance structure may have a number of key partner organizations on a board or committee, or a management or real estate company responsible for managing the building. Still, the Shopping Mall may control the cultural content by the means of a mission and core purpose. It rents out most of its services (bars, restaurants and rehearsal studios) to external organizations. The building is usually owned by the municipality.

The Boutique. A center specialized in a specific art form or activity, and generally smaller than the Department Store or Shopping Mall. It usually has a centralized structure as the Department Store, but with a smaller number of departments and less activities.

The centers in this study have some features of every mentioned model, but most of them fall under either the charity shop or the shopping mall. A cultural center has a business model even if it is not clearly articulated, but as seems to be the general case, there is a need for rethinking and reevaluating the model. The attempts are often shortsighted and are thus not sufficient for effectively advancing the organization in the longer run.

Whether the applied business models really are the best is naturally difficult to determine, since more comparative objects would be needed to be able to draw such conclusions. The cultural centers in this study manage their activities in a somewhat different ways in a mutual comparison, but this has its origins in the characteristics of the different regions rather than in the mutually comparable and strategically different business models. Perhaps the most critical statement that emerged within the framework of this topic was that there is no *"vision for survival"* (Informant C) among the cultural actors, but according to the general results of this study, the centers seem to be aware of the need to develop this side of the organization.

If the resources are scarce, it is even more important to measure and advance the organizations performance and effectiveness from significant dimensions in order to maximize the organizations efficiency (Bardolet and Dhanwani, 2021). At the moment, many organizations consider measurement as a sign of distrust toward the staff – which could not be further from the truth. The difficulties in managing cultural organization tend to depend on the intricacy to determine the value of the intangible and subjective artistic product characteristics. Cultural organizations in general are in a process of economization, and need thus to react on the management discourse that is inflicted upon them. However, how the organization measures itself is an entirely different question. Financial metrics alone are not even particularly effective to measure any other than a cultural organizations performance (Ratnatunga and Montali, 2020), so why would this be enough for cultural centers? The centers need to find different sets of indicators that consider the specific features of their fields. The key performance indicators are not such that can be generalized, every organization need to find these themselves. Naturally some are more apparent than others, such as number of attendees, but others may be connected to a specific arts field or the region. The focus should be on what is to be measured and why, and as expected, how it is measured. What is done with these figures later on is also of upmost importance. They need to lead to a reassessment of the organization.

Evaluations should not either become self-fulfilling measurement, where the cultural organizations merely strive to optimize the performance indicators rather than focusing on their own cultural aims, their real mission (Zembylas, 2019). In addition, permanent efficiency demands seldom pair well with the artistic creativity, this is why the management should be aware of the risk of easily and falsely adapting the goals of evaluations as the sole aim of the organization. Using standardized evaluations may become a fast lane toward institutional isomorphism, a streamlining of the organization with others in the same field (DiMaggio and Powell, 1983). Losing the competitive edge should not be the result of evaluations, since this is fairly the opposite of what a business model aims at.

Even if the business model's state of mind is clearly entering the field of cultural centers, there is clearly still a disagreement between business and arts. A rather persistent clinging on to values fixed in the very opposition between arts and economics was covered in Section 2.1:

> *I want to distinguish between a more … capitalist, rational, utility-based work and the cultural, that […] is rooted in play and aesthetic values and beauty and more of the sublime in some way. So, that's where it's rooted.*

(Informant L)

A question that the cultural center entrepreneurs can ask themselves in the initial stage of founding a cultural center as well as later on, is whether there is a sound economy for the project? What are the market conditions for the culture center in the planned location? As seems to be the case in practice amongst most of the cultural centers in this study, there are many grants to apply in Nordic countries. But the important thing is that when fixing a business plan, the grants should not be used as a backbone to balance the economy. The starting point should be to create a business model based on business operations. The goal should be to define the framework for the intended business and its finances, its conditions and opportunities. To find a solid financial ground to stand on requires more than merely subsidies. A culture center can therefore advantageously and continuously invest resources in rethinking how to manage the economy in order to be able to facilitate arts and culture. A business plan is a very useful tool to do this.

2.3 Building on Arts or Building a Building?

If we had a visitor from the 19th century, he or she would likely feel at home in the cultural buildings of today. They have generally not changed considerably. But with growing costs, how is the society supposed to afford these cultural monuments? Simultaneously, does the society afford not to have them? It is anything but cheap to maintain a building, but lack of cultural stimulus will also be expensive for the society. If further elaborating this contradiction, is there any point in either investing in cheaper buildings (with less attraction and less years ahead) or moneymaking arts and culture (losing the centers cutting edge)? The only certainty, as it seems, is that the cultural centers generally will have to rethink their purpose in order to become more affordable and sustainable, as well as to keep on attracting customers. This chapter will mainly focus on the situation today by examining both the literature as well as the perspective of the informants.

In the past 20 years the society has undergone a major change, mostly due to the virtual possibilities and technological solutions, which inevitably has decreased the interest of the potential attendances in physical cultural spaces (Carbonare & Prokupek, 2021). Accessibility has been emphasized as well as the need for sociability. Traditional cultural spaces with one artistic dimension has as a result been shifted toward multifunctional spaces – something that at least in theory has strengthened or even reinvented the cultural centers. In addition, as the social interaction hardly will decrease, rather the opposite, cultural centers may have an advantage in being "just" a space open for anyone and everything. Most of the centers in focus of this study emphasize just this, being a platform for every kind of creative people and organizations within the field of arts and culture, and by doing so influencing the society at large.

> [We] *want to give artists and activists and creative people a place where they can decide for themselves and where they have access to the resources they require to create creatively. I also believe that it is something that is good for the whole society, and that it can be a counterforce to negative things in society. If you gather a lot of creative people in one place and give them resources for self-determination, I think good things happen.*
>
> (Informant O)

Cultural centers are culture and arts embodied in a specific building. As we often see in society, culture tends to get specific places where to operate, which is somewhat confusing. It is as if the location, the very walls of the building where the cultural activities take place both function as the cause, the definition as well as the limitation of the creative work. Cultural centers may be a physical manifestation of arts and culture taking place, but the very core of the creative work should not be defined or even restricted to the walls set by a center.

> *The problem is that culture is always separated to be in its own place* [...]. *And for us, this is completely ridiculous. Culture needs to be the central pillar if you are to build something that actually has an impact on people's inner well-being and creative ability. Whether the creative ability is used to be an aircraft engineer, or used to be an actor, or painter, as well.*
>
> (Informant K)

Simultaneously, having knowledge about a specific building lowers the threshold for the audience visit. The tie between arts and customer is usually a profoundly local phenomenon (Cuenca et al., 2017). Culture evolves where people come in contact, as in their neighborhoods, in cities, in schools – or at cultural centers. All with the benefit of being close to the customers' homes. This is of course not to say that some visitors would not have other incentives to visit art and cultural events, but it is a considerable reason for the majority of visits. Furthermore, the marketing gets easier with one specific address, as well as the public awareness of such a house that is completely in the use of arts and culture (Informant A). In this way the building actually builds on arts, and not the other way around.

As became somewhat clear in Section 1.1, a cultural center does not customarily have an artistic staff. The focus is rather on facilitating external cultural events taking place within the scope of the cultural center, and thus, the center itself – that is the building – does receive a certain amount of focus by the maintaining organization of the center. With thousands of cultural centers only in Europe, there are however most certainly different motivations as to why the centers exist, and thereby also contrasting reasons to which is more important, the content or the building.

However, the results of this study indicate that particularly the private initiatives among the centers in focus are driven by the urge of working for arts and culture (Informant A; Informant D; Informant K; Informant O), be that participation, freedom of expression, creative encounters or such. As implicated in Section 1.1, public initiatives generally focuses on disseminating the cultural strategy of the municipality, as they function under other (ordinarily political) mechanisms than their private counterparts (Informant M). Still, the public centers more often than not have no greater liability over the building, as there is a separate municipal division administering the real estate issues. On the other hand, the same usually applies to the private initiatives as well, as they tend to operate in their buildings as long-term tenants. Here the responsibility to pay the rent of the venue may however become more burdensome and dominant in comparison to the public centers. This may lead to choosing straightforward cash cow solutions as to the cultural content, in order to manage the economy (Informant B). Thus, focusing on the building more than on arts. Then again, this very pressure may also lead to creating novel solutions to the problem; for instance, projects that not only supports the mission of the center, but which also comes with alternative revenues. The container village on the parking area at the cultural center Blivande in Stockholm, Sweden, is a good example of such a project (read more in Section 3.4).

The majority of the cases in this study represent private cultural centers. Still, there are issues and advantages in managing a public cultural center as well, which involves both arts and the building. Taking quick decisions and reacting to emerging trends may very well be the most important advantage that the private centers have, but at the same time, the opposite of this taking place in the public centers may be their advantage too. As one informant put it nicely:

> *it would not have been so difficult to implement or needed so many decisions, but since the municipal structure looks like it does, it must go a certain way, which sometimes leads to it taking its time. But*

sometimes I can also think that it is nice to work in the municipality, because all decisions go the same process and all decisions are secured in the same way and on the same grounds, which somehow makes it very easy to navigate and it feels like every investment are weighed against each other. So, I think there is a very big advantage to being municipal as well.

(Informant M)

Even if there seems to be quite a clear view about whether the building or the cultural content matters the most (to avoid ambiguity, it shall be affirmed that the cultural content is the right answer), there may be other angles as to why it might not be such a bad idea to consider just which building a cultural center should occupy. If the cultural content is all about being creative, this should also apply to the walls. In fact, probably the biggest social and ecological decision a cultural center organization ever makes is that of which walls they choose to use in their forthcoming activities.

when I was younger, when we simply took over houses that had been completely abandoned and politically, I think it's wrong to ravage the resources on this planet in that way […] invest huge resources in building something in one place and then venture capitalists can come in who basically plunder the place and slaughter the resources and leave behind a ruin. […] That capital abandons a place and leaves gigantic premises behind. They have neglected to maintain them for decades. […] But at the same time, I also see it as an opportunity […] for the cultural initiative to go in and […] take back a place that is collective and good for many and for the society.

(Informant O)

For sure, not all cultural center entrepreneurs are left-wing (supporting the political left; relating to the belief that wealth and power should be shared between all parts of society, (Cambridge Dictionary, 2022)) or political at all, but as the essence of a cultural center focuses on participation, freedom of expression and creative encounters, as well as well-being in the society, the value scale does tip somewhat to what is considered to be political liberalism. This book is however not a political manifestation of any sort, for which reason we will not continue to dwell in this arena. It is nevertheless of importance to understand the underpinnings of the cultural center entrepreneurs in order to accurately recognize the mechanisms behind each one of them. As we could conclude from the citation above, beyond the capitalism versus socialism agenda, there seems to be a genuine concern of sustainability. On both an art, the building and on a societal level.

There is also another aspect to consider when it comes to cultural content and cultural center buildings. That is the split between the landlord and the maintainer of the activities in the center – if these are two separate organizations. This may be a dilemma, particularly if the landlord has an own interest in the cultural offering of the house. An important question to ask is thus who the audience perceive as the owner of the culture center. It is naturally clear that the property owner owns the building, but it should be equally clear in the organizational structure that it is the organization that conducts the business itself that defines the building. As became clear during the interviews especially with the Finnish centers (Informant A; Informant G), a too active property owner may blur the boundaries and create unclarity in the image.

One conclusion to be drawn from this is quite similar to the preceding chapter; there is naturally a need to focus on the building – the very essence of the cultural center – to some extent, but the mission (hopefully focused on how the center can facilitate arts and culture) should always be prioritized.

2.4 Current Issues and Future Directions

During the last years, we have seen many surprising events shaping the current issues of mostly everyone. Both the COVID-19 pandemic and Russia's invasion of Ukraine affect nearly every organization in some way. Then again, these trials shall pass, and other will likely lay ahead. This chapter will not focus – at least entirely – on any specific crisis. Rather on more common issues that may influence future directions.

Even if this chapter aims at dealing with everyday issues, it is naturally clear that the above mentioned trials will affect the upcoming ordinary life – every crisis is normally accompanied by an economical deficit that will have to be dealt with, and rather often we have seen that arts and culture are not as appreciated in the society as we would like to think. Therefore, there will most certainly be a need for increased efficiency on many levels, since both the potential customer spending as well as municipal and private subsidies will most likely diminish as inflation increase. This too will lead to a need for a rethinking amongst the cultural centers.

The requirement of efficiency is not by any means a new development. Even before current crisis, arts and cultural organization mostly all around the world have faced many challenges; governments and municipalities have expressed their desire for the organizations to become more entrepreneurial and thereby acquiring more income sources of their own (Carbonare and Prokupek, 2021). In the wake of this development, they pressure to attract more visitors, to diversify their income sources and providing more appealing cultural content has become ever more ubiquitous. Some organizations have not survived, others have recognized the need to adopt their business models to changing needs and conditions.

Earlier studies in Nordic countries has shown that cultural centers with a more diverse portfolio of revenues, the less any individual revenue source will affect the center if the revenue should diminish (Järvinen, 2021). The center with a vast palette of revenues also has a better possibility to plan ahead, as well as attracting funding at a given moment for future activities (Turrini and Voss, 2021). This emphasizes the need of multi-year planning, and amongst other things it may attract longer-term donors and collaborators as well.

But how do the cultural centers manage their economy? According to Cultural Data (2018) the average earned operating revenues of performing arts centers (cultural centers) in USA are 69.5% of their total turnover. In other words, 30.5% is contributed, either public or private funding. On average, the same figure is 22% amongst European cultural centers, which in turn translates to 78% earned incomes, divided into 34% from rentals, 32% from ticket sales, 24% from catering sales and the rest from sales of services, sponsorship, cloakroom and retail sales (Bogen, 2018).

It must be emphasized that these figures are averages, and by no means do they include all cultural centers of Europe. As could be seen in Chapter 1, the annual turnover of the European centers varies a lot, and so does the contributed income in form of public subsidies. This can be seen amongst the informants in this study as well, since new cultural centers hardly have a better position to negotiate governmental or municipal revenues than the more established and institutionalized arts and cultural organizations. As one informant put it:

> *We had to build a business model, we had to build a company, we had to build a model that would make this work. Because we decided right from the start that we will do this no matter what [...] We could not depend on government support, we could not depend on any kind of philanthropist, we could not depend on always getting project subsidies. We had to build this in such a way that it could go around on its own.*

(Informant K)

As mentioned in Section 2.2, at the very core of having an up-to-date business model is the recognition of the need for bringing value to the customer, sufficient and ongoing planning and making money on the process. Let us dive into these subject closer in the spirit of both current issues for cultural centers as well as future directions.

Bringing value to the customers is anything but an easy task. As is superfluous to declare, there is no consensus in the matter of taste. This is simply a result of many factors in the upbringing of every individual and the influence of their specific society. Nevertheless, this is why it is so important for arts organizations to understand the process of shaping a taste, since that is the key for the organizations to build future audiences for itself. The cultural participation. And as we could see in Section 2.1, the customer, not the cultural content, lies at the core of the centers value proposition (Addis and Rurale, 2021).

It is equally as important to consider that art is an empirical product; it has to be experienced. Therefore, the centers need more information about how the customers experience the visit to an exhibition or a show, attached to the general experience of the encountered service. This in turn can extend their common knowledge of this important element of the artistic product. Variables such as creation and production of the cultural products, distribution and pricing, as well as promoting and raising funds are essential to measure in order to grasp the progress of the organization. Yet, quite often it seems as if this procedure is not done – more enquiries are simply needed.

The cultural centers should aim to know their customer (Carbonare and Prokupek, 2021). This can be done for instance by gathering a database of customers opinions, questions and experiences – a core strategy for analyzing the impact of their cultural offering. Where do the customers live, how do they arrive at the center, are they tourists or local residents? It is even more crucial to have a deeper understanding of the various motivations, ambitions and needs of the customers.

As many cultural centers have done, by providing cafés and additional social meeting points they attract an adult audience. Families in turn may require child-friendly spaces within the center. And thus, the children, being a specifically important target audience representing the future audience. Anything that adds to convenience is added value for the customer.

As mentioned above, the present economic climate where the cultural centers have no choice than using their resources as effectively as possible, simultaneously represents an opportunity to rethink, re-create and innovate and in such a manner bring new value to the customer.

Sufficient planning is at the very core of building a sustainable cultural center. But as Bednáriková (2016) has pointed out, the most essential problem seems to be that cultural centers are lacking both a long-term marketing plan as well as a long-term financial plan. Other researchers have also highlighted the weakness of arts and cultural organizations not using strategic management tools (Reussner, 2003; Bardolet and Dhanwani, 2021). Addis and Rurale (2021) in turn pointed out that COVID-19 revealed that many arts and cultural organizations had inadequate strategies, policies and management processes, as well as a need to entirely rethink the strategies of the institutions.

The idea with strategic planning is to be able to make well-grounded decisions, rather than making ad hoc decisions due to organizational pressures (Sharpen, 2018). Thus, arts and cultural organizations need to define their market. Addis and Rurale (2021) point out that when conceptualizing markets this largely depends on the exchanges taking place between parties. When defining markets, you need to start from the demands.

The thing is that there is an increasing amount of competition and other market challenges in the cultural field beside the transformation of the expectations and needs of the customer (Carbonare and Prokupek, 2021), which inevitably leads to a need to rethink the business models of the cultural centers. In this development the management naturally has a crucial role. All organization have a business model of sorts. But if not well articulated nor designed, merely reproduced of other organizations in the same field, the model will not help – in fact, it is to be considered a risk a cultural center cannot afford to take. In a competitive, market-oriented and ever-changing environment, a cultural center needs to adopt a well-designed, innovative and functional business model to better cope with the challenges.

This book has focused on less than ten-year-old cultural centers. Young arts organizations tend to be smaller, more flexible, nonhierarchical, informal and experimental and maybe even less likely to develop their organization according to structures, planning and formalized ways (Tomka, 2019). This has its benefits when inventing a new approach for the cultural center. But they may even be less prone to use long-term plans.

Still, it seems that all actors in the study have had a clear vision about how the economy should look like in the future. However, almost all have had to adjust their plans along the way and in no way does this diminish the need for a sustainable financial plan. This should be seen as a sign of rethinking and adapting to changes. According to the informants, one should always have a long-term plan in use. This is something that is, of course, both logical and expedient – but as Bogen (2018) reported, 73% of the cultural centers in his study said they had a business model, but when asked to describe it, very few could. The process of rethinking the model regularly has its advantage in keeping the model close to everyday work.

Making money on the process of bringing value to the customers is the other side of the coin of being a cultural center – it is not only about facilitating arts and culture. The net costs for cultural activities need to be weighed against the income that the activities in the house can bring, and the plan needs to include a long-term perspective – the activities will not be profitable immediately.

As to the earlier question of arts or economics (Section 2.1), the informants had a quite clear viewpoint regarding the artists they collaborate with, and their attitude toward dealing with the entrepreneurial side of being an artist. By defining this combination, the informant below simultaneously defines the role of the cultural center as in supporting the artist.

> *to be able to be an artist, you must be a high-performing entrepreneur as well. And there are very many of the best artists who have no aptitude for it at all and no interest in it either. But in order for them to function and work with art, they need to be somewhere. You need equipment.*
>
> (Informant O)

As a part of the planning process, some of the informants pointed out that the culture centers should have the possibility to make deficit at first. Cultural activities are not a gold mine and it takes time to find an economic balance and customers. If you milk the cow too much and too early, there is a risk that the cow will not live too long. The business operator's focus should be on commercial activities, at the same time as the diversity of the cultural offering should force the business operator to balance the ticket price according to presumed consumption. With such measures, a clientele of both temporary tenants and individual customers is created, which gives the business a long-term perspective and thus in the long run also a financial sustainability – something that should have a positive effect even on the property owners. At the same time, it is clear that the actors who run the business in the culture centers move within the business domains when they are engaged in renting space, ticket sales, service production and more. Therefore, the economy should also revolve around commercial profitability – even if there are exceptions in the business that form a basis for, for example, support and grants.

There is naturally a vast amount of issues cultural centers must deal with on a daily basis, many of them being specific to their own region. This chapter has aimed at highlighting some general issues as well as connecting a business model mindset as a future direction to the management of a cultural center as a practical tool. The very essence of a business model is at the end of the day to minimize negative surprises and to focus on the main mission and current issues. By removing ramifications of the mission, a cultural center can aim attention and invest sufficient resources to the main task and thus be more efficient.

Next, we will take a closer look at the cultural center Schaumansalen. They have changed their focus along their way in order to be better equipped to implement their main task. Furthermore, we will present their way of making money on the process of bringing value to the customers.

2.5 Case Presentation: Schaumansalen

As the theme of this chapter is the business approach and the core values, this specific case presentation aims at illustrating one way to go about when combining a sound business with overarching cultural core values. As this chapter addresses the issue of business approach and core values, this case will be presented through these lenses.

2.5.1 A Brief History of Schaumansalen

Schaumansalen (the Schauman Hall) is a part of Campus Allegro, a campus unit consisting of adjoining properties in the heart of Jakobstad in Finland, with a concert hall in the absolute middle of the campus that forms Schaumansalen (Campus Allegro, 2022). The hall, which seats just over 400 spectators, is run by the limited company Jakobstads konsertsal Ab (Schaumanhall, 2022). The company has been active since 2013 when Campus Allegro was inaugurated. Campus Allegro is owned by the Foundation for Åbo Akademi University, while Schaumansalen is owned by Novia University of Applied Sciences. Schaumansalen was created as part of the new campus.

The campus consists of buildings from four different centuries (Campus Allegro, 2022): the oldest house is from 1797, a stone house that was a private residence from the beginning; Lassfolk's wooden building is from the 19th century; Lassfolk's lace factory is from the 20th century, a large brick building; the new commercial part is built in the 2000s (Informant I). The Foundation for Åbo Akademi was the constructor and main guarantor of the project, but many other foundations were also involved (Informant J).

2.5.2 The Organizational Structure

The campus includes the Novia University of Applied Sciences' art and culture educations (music, performing arts, art, photography, design), including basic art education at the Wava Institute, the Federation of Swedish Municipalities in Ostrobothnia for Education and Culture and the YA–Vocational College of Ostrobothnia (Campus Allegro, 2022). There is also another vocational school, called Centria. All actors thus rent their premises from the foundation for Åbo Akademi (Informant H) with their own rental agreements, except for Jakobstads Konsertsal Ab, which rents Schaumansalen directly from Novia University of Applied Sciences (Informant J). There is a campus board with representatives of all tenants where issues that are common to the whole house are dealt with. There are also other collaborative bodies, such as the management group for the music hall, the visual arts, the dramatic arts, as well as the Black box's management group.

Novia University of Applied Sciences is the head of Jakobstads Konsertsal Ab, which means that Novia's principal is chairman of the board; the chairman of Novia as well as a representative of the city of Jakobstad are board members (Schaumanhall, 2022). In addition, there is also a producer that works for Schaumansalen. The limited company has no employees of its own, as those who work for the concert hall are employed by Novia (Informant J), with the exception of stage and wardrobe staff and others working on an hourly basis for the limited company (Informant I).

2.5.3 The Business Model

The original incentive for Schaumansalen was the need for a space for concerts and live music within the framework of the educations (Schaumanhall, 2022). Over the years, however, the space has become more of a cultural living room for the city of Jakobstad and the surrounding area with strong roots in the municipality. At first, the hall largely had its own productions and a CEO who arranged the events, but it was difficult to get profitability in their own productions (Informant I). Nowadays, the company therefore focuses on a variety of operations; they rent out the hall to a much greater extent and arrange their own events to a limited extent. In addition to new tenants, the company has annually returning guests.

The staff of Schaumansalen believe that it would not work to focus solely on commercial rental and content in such a small environment as the city of Jakobstad (Informant J). In such an environment, a culture center needs to have many different models to make money, an entirety that allows both nonprofit and commercial actors to provide cultural content. In this way, the broad cultural life of the region is included in the center and the center becomes somewhat of a cultural hub. As such, the center strives to balance between their main goals of staying true to their core value of being an enabler of arts and culture in the region, as well as having a sound economy.

During a normal (non-pandemic) financial year, for example 2018 or 2019, approximately 110–130 events are arranged in the hall. Of these, about 10 are arranged by Jakobstads Konsertsal Ab (Informant J). Examples of such own events are several Schaumansalen Digital LIVE concerts, classical music evenings and concerts as well as an all-singing concert in the time of Advent. In addition, one can see about 60%–70% of the total number of events (about 66–91) as some form of co-productions, since the hall's producers participate in the work prior to these events. Examples of major co-productions are festivals such as the Allegro Spring Festival (organizer Pro allegro rf), the Chamber Music Festival RUSK (organizer Jakobstads Sinfonietta), Jeppis Jazz Festival (organizer Jazzoo rf) and Runebergsveckan (the city of Jakobstad being the organizer). All of these are several-day events consisting of a diverse range of cultural content, where the producer of Jakobstads Konsertsal Ab actively collaborates with the directors of the festivals.

According to the informants, the own events are both substantively and financially considered initiatives (Informant J). The goal of the company's own production is to broaden the hall's cultural content offerings, which is why they also emphasize the importance of the grants they receive – they enable a varied content.

Jakobstads Konsertsal Ab company's finances are divided into five categories:

1   the educational actors in Campus Allegro who continuously rent the space,
2   the city that rents sixty evenings a year for local actors,
3   the external customers that rent the hall,
4   the operational support from Finnish-Swedish foundations, and
5   the staff of Novia University of Applied Sciences working for the hall (Informant J).

There is also a support association called Pro Allegro (Jakobstads Konsertsal Ab, 2021). The association consists of cultural volunteers who started this activity at an early stage after the hall had been built

(Informant I). The association is a contact link to both local users, audiences and consumers, and the purpose of the association is to be able to provide both content support and concrete help to the activities in the whole campus, but usually focused on the concert hall. The funding model for universities in Finland include publication activities, which in artistic university areas are seen as artistic productions (Informant J). As the hall's producer is employed by the polytechnic school Novia, the productions that the producer produces can be included in the university's annual publication. Thus, YH Novia receives government funding for annually notified productions, which in turn helps to cover the producer's salary.

As Figure 2.1 shows, Schaumansalen has a fairly focused and clear financial environment, where Jakobstads Konsertsal Ab fully focuses on the task of maintaining the activities in the culture center, while the surrounding organizations and actors support that task in various ways.

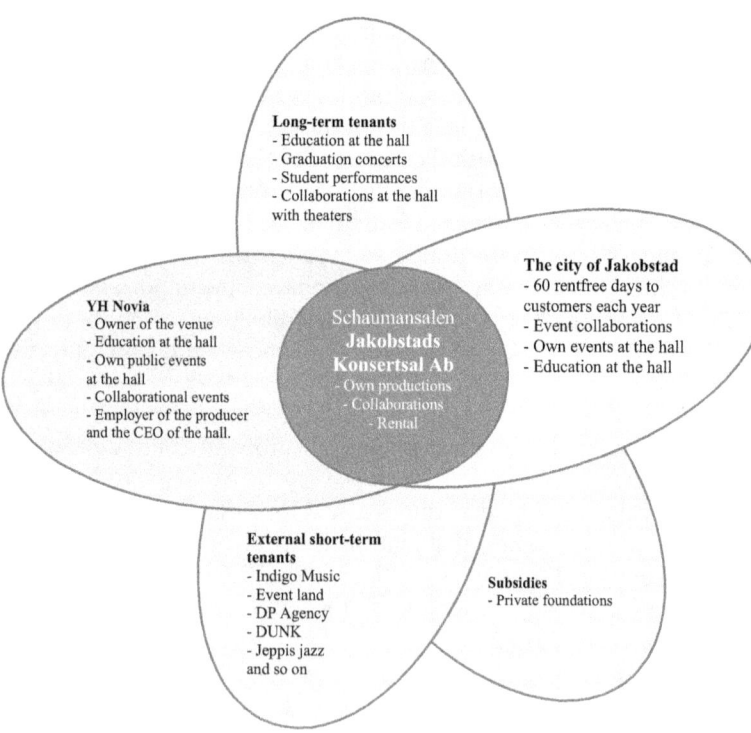

Figure 2.1 The economic environment of Schaumansalen.

Their business model is thus relatively evenly distributed between these five areas, and so are the revenues of these areas too. It both offers a versatile financial foundation for Schaumansalen, as well as a versatile offering of culture.

Jakobstads Konsertsal Ab sees itself as being equally a culture center, a concert hall and an education hall (Informant J). It can also be read as them having a sound balance between their regional possibilities of earning revenues while simultaneously actualizing their core mission of enabling arts and culture.

2.6 Summary and Conclusions

The debate about arts and economics, business and core values will most likely thrive even further on, irrespective of what this book has laid forth. The aim of this chapter has nevertheless been to highlight the alternative perspectives on this dilemma. Or that is to say, to neglect calling it a dilemma altogether. It should rather be perceived as a natural order and a possibility to further enhance the facilitation of arts and culture by accepting the necessity of economic awareness.

The focus on making money can certainly weaken the cultural content production, which in turn can be distorted into a repetitive product without any connection to creative work. However, the same applies in the opposite direction of business operations. It can prove difficult to create profitability if the artistic goals are to be the sole governing mechanisms. The dichotomy between art and business should be seen as a balance, as with everything else: both are needed to succeed. Cultural organizations simply need to be cost-effective and strive to diversify their sources of funding and streamline administrative structures to ensure financial stability – without being driven solely by financial interests.

The same applies to the opposition between arts and buildings. The buildings may be hard to maintain, but given such incommensurable support to the creative work that it could be concluded that the pros outweigh the cons. None of the informants saw the building as anything else than a platform for supporting arts and culture.

Using tools such as business models has traditionally not been well received in the cultural sector, mostly due to reluctance toward the concept of business. The goal of a business model is nevertheless to create a clear and distinct plan for the organization's business operations and a basis for investigating opportunities for future development. The cultural centers should be ambitious enough in their operations to withstand competition – for the centers are surely enough a part of a competitive market. Cultural centers need therefore to guarantee commercial viability in order to ensure the implementation of their cultural and in a broader sense social task.

The aim has not been to compile a survival guide for cultural centers in the midst of COVID-19 pandemic or eastern European wars. Still, besides leaving tormented and more fragile societies behind them, these trials will have tested us all (granted, some way more than others). Arts and cultural organizations that have not been in tune with the demands of their societies and/or have had unsustainable business models or economies, will most likely perish – if they have not already.

2.7 Practical Recommendations

- Arts and economics should not be contradicted as an either-or question; it is rather about being efficient. How to consider the need for a sustainable economy in order to continue facilitating arts and culture.
- As the audience is overwhelmed with alternative leisure time entertainment, cultural centers have to rethink their approach and be more entrepreneurial – while still staying true to their values and mission.
- A business model is about having a strategy for assessing the market, evaluating the successes and failures and predicting the future for the sake of staying ahead of the inevitable competition. A practical tool for managing a cultural center.
- The goal for a cultural center should be to define the framework for the intended business and its finances, its conditions and opportunities.
- There should be a focus on the building – the very essence of the cultural center – but the mission should be prioritized, but not excessively.
- Direct funding support is not always the most important form of support arts cultural centers receive from local authorities.

Application Exercise

Choose a cultural center (or any other arts organization within the same framework as your organization) that has dealt with a value discussion including the question about arts and economics. You should really not have to try that hard – almost every organization within arts and culture should be applicable. Analyze that organization; their perceived need for the value discussion, which measures were taken, which results did it lead to and how did it affect the staff?

References

Addis, M., & Rurale, A. (2021). A Call to Revise Cultural Business Management. In: *Managing the Cultural Business. Avoiding Mistakes, Finding Success*. Ed: Addis, M. & Rurale, A. New York: Routledge, pp. 1–31.

Adorno, T. (1991). *The Culture Industry*. New York: Routledge.

Amit, R., & Zott, C. (2012). Creating value through business model innovation. *Sloan Management Review*, 53(3), pp. 41–49.

Bardolet, D., & Dhanwani, R. (2021). Agile Management in the Arts. The Mistake of Over-improvisation. In: *Managing the Cultural Business. Avoiding Mistakes, Finding Success*. Ed.: Addis, M & Rurale, A. New York: Routledge, pp. 111–142.

Bednáriková, D. (2016). Culture Center as a Universal and Sustainable Public Culture Space. In: *Cultural Management Education in Risk Societies–Towards a Paradigm and Policy Shift?! Conference Proceedings 2016*. Ed.: Imperiale, F. & Vecco, M. ENCATC, pp. 4–14. Accessed: 12.1.2022, available at: https://encc.eu/sites/default/files/2016-10/ENCATC_AC_Book_2016.pdf

Bienkowski, P. (2019). *Do volunteers still have a place in museums and cultural organizations?* Apollo. The international Art Magazine. Accessed: 25.1.2022, available at: www.apollo-magazine.com/volunteers-museums-cultural-organisations/

Bogen, P. (2018). *Stronger Arts and Cultural Organisations for a Greater Social Impact. Business Models Profiling of Cultural Centres & Performing Arts Organisations*. Sweden: Trans Europe Halles, Creative Lenses.

Cambridge Dictionary (2022). *The left wing*. Homepage. Accessed: 8.8.2022, available at: https://dictionary.cambridge.org/dictionary/english/left-wing.

Campus Allegro (2022). *Campus Allegro*. Homepage. Accessed: 5.8.2022, available at: https://campusallegro.fi/om-campus-allegro/

Carbonare, P. M. D., & Prokupek, M. (2021). Cultural Business Models. The Mistake of Obsoletion. In: *Managing the Cultural Business. Avoiding Mistakes, Finding Success*. Ed.: Addis, M., & Rurale, A. New York: Routledge, pp. 32–77.

Chesbrough, H. (2011). *Open Services Innovation*. San Fransisco: JosseyBass.

Cuenca, M., Poprawski, M., Righolt, N., Silvaggi, A., Tolosa, I., Torreggiani, A., Goodacre, J., & Vidovic, D. (2017). *Study on Audience Development. How to Place Audiences at the Centre of Cultural Organisations. Executive Summary*. European Union. Accessed at: 23.3.2022, available at: http://engageaudiences.eu/files/2017/04/EX-summary-NC-04-16-496-EN-N.pdf

Cultural Data (2018). *Key Takeaways: What We Learned.* Website. Homepage. Accessed: 24.3.2022, available at: https://culturaldata.org/reports/earned-operating-revenue/key-takeaways/

DeVereaux, C. (2019). Introduction. In: *Arts and Cultural Management. Sense and Sensibilities in the State of the Field.* Ed.: DeVereaux, C.. New York: Routledge, pp. xix–xxx.

DiMaggio, P., & Powell, W. (1983). The iron cage revisited: Institutional isomorphism and collective rationality in organizational fields. *American Sociological Review,* 48(2), pp. 147–160.

Drucker, P. (1954). *The Practice of Management.* New York: Harper & Row.

Eikhof, D. R., & Haunschild, A. (2007). For art's sake! Artistic and economic logics in creative production. *Journal of Organizational Behavior,* 28(5), pp. 523–538.

Falk, J. H., & Shepard, B. (2006). *Thriving in the Knowledge Age: New Business Models for Museums and Other Cultural Institutions.* Lanham, MD: Rowman Altamira.

Frey, B. S. (2003): *Arts & Economics: Analysis & Cultural Policy.* New York: Springer.

Germain-Thomas, P. (2019). Arts Marketing. A New Marketing Art. In: *Arts and Cultural Management. Sense and Sensibilities in the State of the Field.* Ed.: DeVereaux, C. New York: Routledge, pp. 152–166.

Jakobstads Konsertsal Ab (2021). *Verksamhetsberättelse 2020.* PDF Document. Accessed: 5.8.2022, available at: www.dropbox.com/s/q15abj4fgc0yr7k/verksamhetsberattelse2020.pdf?dl=0

Järvinen, T. (2021): *Strategic Cultural Center Management.* New York: Routledge.

Magretta, J. (2002). Why business models matter. *Harvard Business Review,* 80(5), pp. 86–92.

Mangset, P. (1995). Risks and benefits of decentralization: The development of local cultural administration in Norway. *The European Journal of Cultural Policy,* 2(1), pp. 67–86.

McCall, K. (2019). The Reality of Cultural Work. In: *Arts and Cultural Management. Sense and Sensibilities in the State of the Field.* Ed.: DeVereaux, C. New York: Routledge, pp. 167–184.

Osterwalder, A., & Pigneur, Y. (2010). *Business Model Generation: A Handbook for Visionaries, Game Changers and Challengers.* New York: John Wiley & Sons.

Ratnatunga, J., & Montali, L. (2020). *Performance Management Measures.* In: *Strategic Management Accounting (4th Edition).* Ed.: Ratnatunga, J. Melbourne: Quill Press, pp. 405–426.

Reussner, E. M. (2003). Strategic management for visitor-oriented museums. A change of focus. *International Journal of Cultural Policy* 9(1), pp. 95–108.

Schaumanhall (2022). *Jakobstads konsertsal Ab.* Homepage. Accessed: 5.8.2022, available at: https://schaumanhall.fi/jakobstadskonsertsalab/.

Shafer, S. M., Smith, H. J., & Linder, J. C. (2005). The power of business models. *Business Horizons,* 48, pp. 199–207.

Sharpen, C. (2018). *Why Strategy Fails in Arts Organizations*. Sharpen Creative Industries Consulting. Accessed: 24.1.2022, available at: www.sharpencic. com.au/brings-pain-to-purdue-pharma-bankruptcy-hearings-in-new-york

Teece, D. J. (2010). Business models, business strategy and innovation. *Long Range Planning*, 43(30), pp. 172–194.

Throsby, D. C. (2010). *The Economics of Cultural Policy*. Cambridge, UK: Cambridge University Press.

Tobelem, J.-M. (2018). Are Cultural Sites Leisure Businesses? In: *Culture, Innovation and the Economy*. Ed.: Mickov, B., & Doyle, J.E. New York; Routledge, pp. 84–97.

Tomka, G. (2019). The Orthodoxy of Cultural Management Research and Possible Paths beyond It. In: *Arts and Cultural Management. Sense and Sensibilities in the State of the Field*. Ed.: DeVereaux, C. New York: Routledge, pp. 108–128.

Turrini, A., & Voss, Z. (2021). Strategic Fundraising in the Arts. The Mistake of Selling. In: *Managing the Cultural Business. Avoiding Mistakes, Finding Success*. Ed.: Addis, M., & Rurale, A. New York: Routledge, pp. 280–310.

Zembylas, T. (2019). Why Are Evaluations in the Fiels of Cultural Policy (Almost Always) Contested? Major Problems, Frictions, and Challenges . In: *Arts and Cultural Management. Sense and Sensibilities in the State of the Field*. Ed.: DeVereaux, C. New York: Routledge, pp. 129–151.

Zott, C., Amit, R., & Massa, L. (2011). The business model: Recent developments and future research. *Journal of Management*, 37(4), pp. 1019–1042.

3 New Nordic Initiatives Paving the Way for New Solutions

It seems as if many cultural centers feel they cannot afford the luxury of rethinking their purpose whilst hectically trying to realize their (sometimes very outdated) mission statement. By no means are the Nordic cultural centers unique in the matter of both resisting the status quo and the institutional pressure of the field, rather they simply constitute the focus cases of this study and are thus presented to some extent in a more positive light – the aim with this book being to highlight successful measures. However, procrastination and retrograde steps do happen in the north of Europe also. This book does focus on Nordic cultural centers, but more accurately on less than ten-year-old centers. Organizations that have proven to be resilient, but most likely not been a subject to institutional pressures just yet. In time, these too will most likely become institutionalized – although maybe in another way than earlier cultural centers.

Institutionalization is the process by which organizations becomes institutions, as these do not emerge in a vacuum. New organizations are compelled to build on both existing technologies, existing ideas, as well as social routines, and will thus consistently echo their institutional influence to some degree (Scott, 2014).

It usually happens as the organization over time is drenched with value *beyond the technical requirements of the task at hand* (Selznick, 1957, p. 17). The processes of institutionalization generally have a conflicting effect on organizational success in the long run (DiMaggio and Powell, 1983). Institutionalization does foster organizational stability and continuity, but it also brings about inflexibility and resistance to change. Correspondingly, once successful, organizations may lose their competitive advantage over time.

Even if the field of cultural centers – both public and private – is quite young, such a stagnation seems to have occurred, where the existing models for administration seldom get challenged (Järvinen,

DOI: 10.4324/9781003253440-3

2021). Still, some new initiatives in Finland and Sweden seem to have taken up the task of rethinking the concept of a cultural center. Not to say that such rethinking would not occur elsewhere, but in this book, we do – as mentioned many times – focus on the Nordic initiatives. And how does these differ from the earlier models and are there something worth considering elsewhere too?

This chapter will start off by analyzing the adaptive cultural center, look into how to organize a center, whereafter take a step further in the development of a healthy center, present a case before finishing with a summary and conclusions.

Chapter Learning Objectives

After reading this chapter, you should have gained knowledge about:

- Founding a new cultural center
- Maintaining an existing cultural center
- What an adaptive cultural center is
- The benefits of an having an adaptive attitude
- Pointers as to how to organize a center and why it is beneficial
- Pointers as to how to take a step further

3.1 Founding a New Cultural Center

There are naturally many incentives for entrepreneurs to found a new cultural center, as there are differing possibilities to do so. This section will not present general exact solutions, although a stepwise guideline with some indicators good to consider is introduced.

Before looking into these indicators, it would be of interest to examine the motivational force behind the six examined cultural centers in this study. A curious difference between them is that they seem to have had quite different reasons to be founded. In Jakobstad, the educational actors have played a central role in the founding of Campus Allegro and the Schaumansalen, with flanked support from the city of Jakobstad and the Foundation for the Åbo Academy (Stiftelsen för Åbo Akademi). The idea was to gather different schools under one roof and share the resources. In Karis, the property owner of the former cultural building Tryckeriteatern, that is, the Foundation for Culture and Education Investments (Stiftelsen för kultur–och utbildningsinvesteringar, SKUI), took an initiative for a new building as it was discovered that the old property was in poor condition. However, the idea was from the beginning to create a common platform for the other actors in the region that may have use of more space in the future. In Helsinki, the initiative was completely independent of existing organizations, with three individual initiators who had a vision of a new Finnish-Swedish district in Helsinki with different services and a cultural center. In Varberg, the initiative came from the municipal, while the idea was to combine the local library, theater and arts hall. Ifö Center was initialized as a platform for collective workshops for and by professional artists, initially renting a part of the old ceramic factory Ifö Ceramics, later on buying the facilities through a crowdfunding campaign. Blivande in turn was founded as a participant-driven scene for participatory art, with the main idea for creative people getting involved in a participatory culture having the possibility to aid when encountering challenges in the society. Although different backgrounds, the basic idea of bringing different actors and organizations under one roof can be detected.

According to the informants, a culture center should be the natural meeting place in the town, centrally located, easy to find and attractive to visit. The range should be wide enough so that everyone, regardless of demographic background or previous experience, can find something that concerns them, but also something they do not know will affect them yet as customers. The cultural center should contribute to growth on several levels; partly by being a meeting place that enables exchanges between people and activities, partly as a place that inspires initiatives and ideas amongst individuals and organizations – especially between those who gather in the center, but also among others active in the region. The cultural center should not compete with existing activities but be created as a complement and/or support function for existing actors.

There are a handful of key factors to focus on when taking the initiative for a new center, factors that rarely get the attention they deserve. For instance, it is important to reflect on "*what similar organizations exist, in what way do we differ from them,* [...] *is there a sufficient foundation and is our profile clear enough*" (Informant B). When it comes to planning new culture centers, the informants have some advice to give. Many of the things they bring forth are certainly not surprising or that new, but yet important. For instance, considering which tenants will use the center and which customers it will attract, and to do a financial plan before the construction begins.

> *I would develop the planned content at a very early stage, determining who are the main actors, that they are involved in the process from beginning to end and not included at a later stage. I think that is the*

most important thing, and of course that they have a financial plan for what this would look like.

(Informant A)

A new building for a new culture center is also not the only model available – it is quite possible to use existing spaces. This is actually the most common solution on a European level (Järvinen, 2021). Something that an informant also emphasized, namely that *you do not build a culture center, but you use existing spaces that are no longer used for what they were built for* (Informant I).

Something that most of the culture centers in this study have experience of is collaboration with the municipalities, and therefore it is natural to emphasize the role of the municipalities in the future. Almost each of the centers show examples of very different solutions on collaborating with the municipality, but what they all have in common is that the collaboration plays an important role for them. In addition, the informants emphasize the importance of local involvement amongst cultural entrepreneurs.

> *it is important that you have a good recognition from the municipality [...], and it may not have so much to do with you wanting grants from them – which is difficult today, but it is about city planning change, it applies to planning issues, it concerns the infrastructure, and then a municipality can come and rent space [...] it is important that there is, so to speak, a local involvement of a number of people, associations, who actually [...] have a genuine interest.*

(Informant E)

It also appears as if the location-specific differences are an important factor to consider. If the region already has theaters or music halls, it is of course much more difficult for a new culture center to stand out. The idea is to look at it site-specifically, considering the local infrastructure in terms of cultural offerings and activities and what existing houses there already can be found.

The comments of the informants can be extracted into the following eight points, presented in Figure 3.1. Note that not only the order of the points can vary, also the points themselves in that each organization, region and cultural center have its own features.

Making of a need's analysis. Something that emerges clearly in this study is that the culture center should respond to a need. However, this is naturally dependent on the size of the region – the smaller the region,

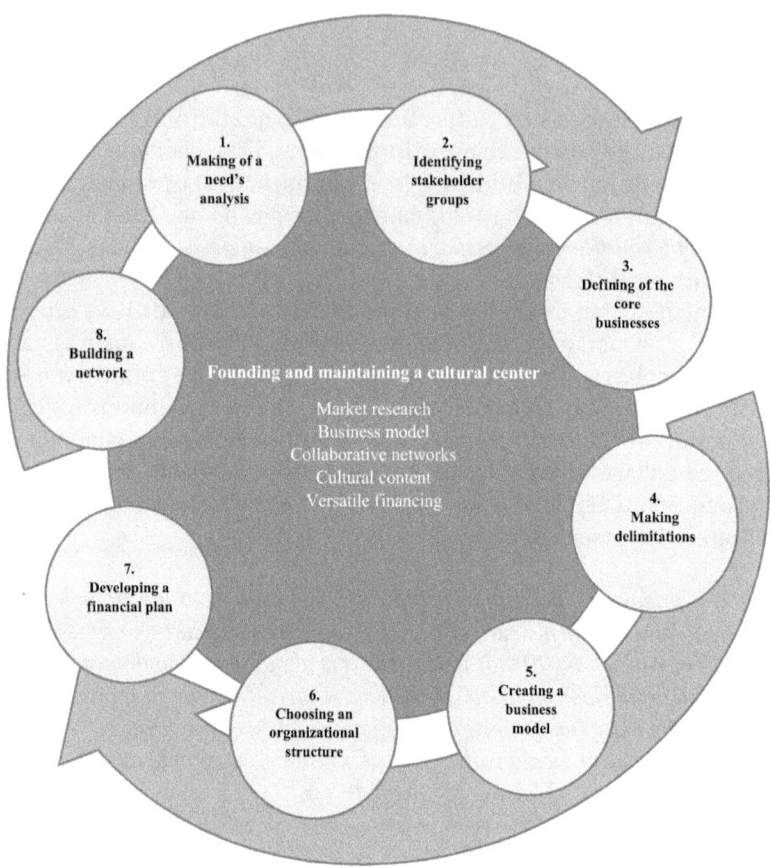

Figure 3.1 The founding and maintenance of a culture center.

less people expressing the need. Therefore, the need can be discovered via the local actors, but also from actors such as the financiers or other individuals and organizations that have noted a need from, for example, a language policy perspective. An important question to ask oneself is that how will the cultural center work in relation to the surrounding society and other actors, what added value does it bring and what void does the center fill?

The needs analysis can advantageously be linked to an analysis of the surrounding society. Regardless of the approach, however, there should be local actors that can run the business and maintain the property in the future. The aim is to identify a demand for the culture center regardless of the level the initiative comes from, and to analyze what need there is for a culture center in that specific location.

Identifying stakeholder groups. Based on the assignment and the objectives, it is important to identify relevant partners in the region. This study has shown evidence of a variety of solutions; educational actors, active arts organizations, municipal actors and individuals. These stakeholders can operate at different levels; as co-financier and maintainer of property and operations (e.g., the municipality in Kulturhuset Fokus), long-term tenants in the office department (e.g., the organizations in Kvarteret Victoria), long-term tenants who also conduct activities on stage (e.g., the Wawa Institute in Schaumansalen/Campus Allegro).

The aim should be to build a cultural consortium instead of (only) creating a new cultural actor among the existing in the area. In addition, it is important to maintain openness to new actors and collaborations, and to investigate opportunities for resource savings through collaborations. The organizations that maintain the activities can favorably involve competent cultural figures and other experts on their boards.

The goal is also to find stakeholders that can maintain a diversity of activities in the center by supporting and complementing the already existing cultural offerings of the region and contribute to a sustainable economy through, for example, permanent (and temporary) rental conditions.

Defining of the core businesses. It is worth noting that there is no one model of culture centers, there are infinitely many; the core activities must reflect the needs and strengths of the locality and the region, an interplay between local actors and an attempt to fill a void. In Jakobstad there was a rich music life and education in the area, ergo the Schaumansalen focused on music. In Karis, there was a need for space for theater activities and therefore the cultural center Fokus focused on theater in the upcoming center. In Bromölla there were individual artists that needed a space, therefore Ifö Center.

In addition to the abovementioned examples, there is also the opportunity to plan support functions around the cultural center, such as a restaurant. In collaboration with the municipality, libraries, museums or, for example, schools can also be placed within the framework of the building and thus be a part of the core business. The activities of the future private tenants should also shape the future culture center. A center that strives to meet the needs of citizens should therefore have a citizen dialogue on the issue of future activities. The regional cultural policy should be analyzed continuously.

The aim is to analyze in advance which services and products will be in focus, in order to then be able to meet the needs these activities pose when founding the center and when formulating the business plan.

Making delimitations. In each process, the purpose of the project needs to form a starting point for determining boundaries and identifying which investments are sustainable. Factors that, among other things, should be carefully assessed in advance are the conditions of the proposed location (audience data, partners), the linguistic situation (e.g., Finland is a bilingual country), an inventory of already existing cultural spaces in the region (how much need there is for yet another venue), the relationship between public and private (is the municipality or private organizations possible partners), spatial and organizational delimitation (room program), financial opportunities (e.g., room program in relation to potential income) and the location (in relation to the intended audience and tenants). The net costs for cultural activities need to be weighed against the revenues that the activities in the center can bring, and the plan needs to consider a long-term perspective – the activities will not be profitable immediately.

An important question to ask is for what main purpose will the culture center exist? In addition, new and already existing actors in the field of cultural centers should constantly engage in self-criticism and scrutiny of their activities, that is rethinking their mission and businesses.

The aim is to define by delimitating the framework for the intended business and its finances, its conditions and opportunities.

Creating a business model. As mentioned in Section 2.2, a business plan is a theoretical description of how an organization or a business is intended to function. Culture is usually not very lucrative, but without a clear business model, the economic balance will most certainly suffer. A culture center benefits from a clearly formulated and articulated business model. As a house with diverse activities, the danger is that the focus becomes too broad instead of focusing on the cultural centers basic mission.

Furthermore, the Business Model Canvas is an effective tool to present, analyze and develop business models (Osterwalder and Pigneur, 2010). It consists of nine different parts that the culture center should have in mind:

Table 3.1 The nine points of the Business Model Canvas.

Value proposition	How does the culture center create value for its customers?
Customer relations	Which services do the customers of the center want and how do you supply these?
Customer segment	All available information about the culture center's different customer segments.
Distribution	How do the services of the center benefit customers?
Stakeholders	What are the characteristics of your most important partners?
Key activities	Everything that is crucial for the culture center to be able to deliver.
Key resources	The crucial resources and capabilities needed to be able to deliver.
Costs	The different types of costs the culture center has.
Revenues	The different revenues the center has.

The entrepreneurs can ask themselves what is the probability for a sustainable economy in the project? What are the market conditions for the culture center in the planned location? The starting point should be a business model that is based on and balances with the business operations. A culture center is a unit that may partly be located within the framework of nonprofit, but for the most part within business activities (as when selling services or renting venues). Therefore, the culture centers compete with other actors in the field of entertainment and culture, and should be ambitious enough to compete.

The goal of a business model is to create a clear and distinct plan for the organization's business operations and a basis for analyzing opportunities for future development.

Choosing an organizational structure. The organizational structure can rightly vary from center to center, depending on the underlying mechanisms that constitute the specific collaboration that occurs in the culture center. This study has mostly presented a model in which ownership and activity have been separated – something that has its advantages in times of crisis such as the COVID-19 pandemic. In such, any organization is something of a house of cards, but by separated ownership and maintenance, there are some benefits; when the top cards fall over, the ones in the bottom may still be left standing for a while. That moment, however short it may be, can prove to be crucial for the property owner.

The cultural center organization should be structured so that the maintaining organization can ensure that the center is used in such a way that the purpose and vision of the culture center is achieved and that it is possible to create financial sustainability over time. This organization should have a coordinating function in the work of linking the core activities and the collaborating organizations. The organization should preferably, in addition to its own activities, fill the house with activities by renting out the premises to external actors and organizers, both commercial and nonprofit, and be responsible to support the activities in the center, be they internally or externally produced. If there are support functions such as restaurants within the organizational structure, these should preferably be at this level in the organizational structure. The owner of the building should rightly focus only on the building.

This study makes no strong arguments for a specific organizational form; there are different strengths with different forms of organization. The point of the organizational form, however, should be that it supports a sustainable economy based on the business activities and provides resilience to sudden changes.

Developing a financial plan. When the previous six points in the proposed figure (Figure 3.1) have been ticked off, the matter of financing should be dealt with. Why this late in the process? It is naturally possible to deal with this matter earlier, but at the same time there is no point in developing a financial plan unless the planned activities has been concretized at a level where the needs have been mapped, the stakeholder groups identified, the core activities defined, the delimitation made, the business model created and the organizational structure completed.

Only then should the culture center entrepreneurs practically work with a financial plan. As the examples in the study have shown (and will show), the finances can be built up in very many different ways. The municipality can contribute a large part (assuming that it subsequently owns a proportionately equal part of the building as with the cultural center Fokus), the property or properties can be built as a financial investment by the owner who then receives the rent needed to pay off the investment, it can involve loans that in the long run is paid off with the help of the external tenants. The models are many.

The biggest costs a culture center has is the building (either the rent or the cost of maintaining the property) and the operating costs. The rental cost is determined on the basis of the total investment cost for the culture center, which is why this must be considered already when planning the investment (if the house is to be built). Operating costs consist primarily of personnel costs as well as communication and marketing. The higher the real estate investment costs, the less room for the cultural content. Therefore, it is of utmost importance that the real estate investment is in proportion to the scope and productivity of the business.

Building a network. Collaboration should be the culture centers guiding light and take place on many different levels; with the centers actors (tenants), the region's other cultural actors, other cultural centers, various organizations that promote culture, the municipality and with the financiers. The cultural center should act as a hub and maintain a dialogue on all levels.

There should be a genuine, clear and unique concept for the cooperation between the various activities in the culture center. A concept that facilitates cooperation and coexistence under one roof, which contributes to different cultural and art forms being brought together, both inspiring and challenging each other. The same applies to the organizations and other actors at the culture center. An added value in the unifying platform such as a culture center, is specifically the opportunity for collaborations it creates.

By collaborating, the aim is to achieve common benefits in program content, knowledge and resource savings – to keep up to date with the field and the trends. It is also beneficial to keep in close contact with the financiers to avoid surprising situations in both directions.

This rounds up the section of founding a new cultural center, so let us now move on to the adaptivity of a cultural center.

3.2 The Adaptive Cultural Center

It is a volatile, ambiguous and complicated world out there today, and this applies especially to the arts. In order to achieve the set goals, it is no longer enough only to build on earlier successes, to plan rationally and to bet on the future echoing the past. If an organization sticks with old approaches as their way to navigate complexity, it is likely that success will escape them and eventually they will fail. *Best practice is yesterday's shit* (Rehn, 2003). Organizational leaders and arts managers need a brand-new mindset and a set of tools to triumph in these circumstances, in order to be able to do more than only react randomly to unpredictable incidents.

Innovation and adaption have become something of a necessity for arts and cultural organizations. Managers of cultural centers need to be intensely aware of the abundant different forces that may have an impact on their organization. The idea with this section is not to present to the reader the exact steps to take to achieve success, rather to highlight matters to be aware of and the mindset that should be cultivated. The surviving organization will most likely be the adaptive organization that identifies changes in the external environment and responds to these effectively while staying true to its mission (Byrnes, 2022).

Changes cannot be avoided, but in order to make the changes successful, valuable and momentous, it is of importance to maintain an adaptive attitude toward the changes (Kotter, 1996). An adaptive organization furthermore has better probabilities of gaining new resources. These organizations tend to focus more on human capabilities rather than their limitations. The adaptive organization is capable to regulate new or relocate existing resources as required to resolve economic difficulties and to focus on arising needs. Adaptability involves focusing on the future, being able to respond to change, being adept and to embrace progress (Fjeldstad et al., 2012). The cultural center that can maximize the present, take advantage of existing ideas and exploit the markets is agile and will most likely be rewarded with a considerable competitive advantage.

As a part of the experience industry, the culture centers are in contact with current social developments (Silvanto et al., 2008). As the environment changes, these organizations need to change their method of approach. And this have evidently been happening also. According to a study on European cultural centers and performing arts organizations (BOP Consulting, 2018), most of these organizations changed their key business practices during the last five years before the study, mostly (1) in the use of digital technology in marketing and communication or internal processes, (2) in increasing the number and width of co-productions, co-marketing and other cooperation partnerships and (3) in the means to generate income or to obtain public or private funding.

Cultural centers, just as any arts organization, should naturally not line up too close with other organizations in the field, with every norm in the field, since a distinction between organizations in the same sector is healthy (Kerrigan and Draeby, 2021). When describing the reality of the changing performing arts industry, Kenneth Foster (2010) accentuates the adaptive organization:

> *Along with innovation comes the need for bold thinking – not just the crazy new ideas we might generate but the systems and procedures to bring those ideas to fruition – to make innovation happen and happen continuously in order to become an adaptive arts organization, one*

that responds to the times and presages for the rest of the culture, what is to come.

(p. 16)

But what about the cases in this study? Given the changes and challenges for activities of the performing arts sectors – especially that of cultural centers, there seems to be a sense of adaptability among the six cases. Each and every one of them has aimed at becoming what the environment has a need for – in many cases even before the need is articulated. When the circumstances have changed, so has the approach of the centers.

When aiming at being adaptive, the organization needs to rethink the whole approach as to what it is doing. There may be an existing theorized and institutionalized model for a cultural center, but that does not mean that it would not be possible to redefine the frame of this model. When having the opportunity to take over a parking space outside the center, the team of Blivande did not limit themselves to what such an area normally should be used to. They let the parking space be adapted to the shortage of space within the center, and started building a container city there to house different artists and other actors that could build upon the cultural centers creative and cultural content. As one of the informants of that very center put it:

> *then we had the opportunity to annex a parking space, on which we started to build our containers. And then we realized that we are not just building a creative artist center, we are building an ecosystem here of people who work together and go far beyond art. […] when we say that it is a culture hub or a creative hub, we think of culture in the broadest sense, as a society in culture. We are trying to build a new kind […], an alternative culture bubble in Stockholm, which still interacts with society.*
>
> (Informant K)

Being adaptive may very well be the niche of the cultural center. Being able to tap into different and sudden opportunities presents a favorable circumstance in relation to their public peers – even if they lack the economic stability.

> *We have something called the idea center, which is a kind of hub, you could say, where young people up to the age of 25 can turn for help to carry out their own cultural events. […] I have never seen it in any other municipality.*
>
> (Informant N)

How does the cultural center manage being adaptive in the long run? This study shows that the managers need to be aware of the various different forces in the society that can have an impact on their center. As any organizations, the centers feel the impact of the economic environment. When the economy is good, this usually tends to reflect on the center. The same applies naturally when the economy is struggling. Both political and demographic issues affect the cultural center as well; being aware of local and national political decisions, lawmaking and the people who live in the region can affect such everyday activities as attendance, programming, ticket prize and donations. A common thread is to listen to the society, in order to be able to predict in which direction things will evolve. If we would like to present this by the means of existing theories, strategic thinking would be one choice. According to Kerrigan and Draebye (2021), strategic thinking is the process defining how people think about, evaluate, view and create the future. It is about the future, but it naturally happens today.

The following section will focus on how to organize the center.

3.3 Organizing the Center

It is of some importance how the organization is organized, as cultural organizations rarely have anything but scarce resources. Thus, such organizations need to be cost-effective. Still, it may be difficult for managers of cultural centers to be objective when structuring the management process of their organization (Fitzgerald, 2008). This may be due to the hope of not being challenged as a leader or of following a personal dream. Nevertheless, good arts managers understand that all enterprises are team efforts. Therefore, cultivating a team approach, making use of individual abilities and utilizing the creativity of many is destined to have a more favorable result. In practice, this could be done by introducing periodic team meetings, encouraging personal development and never neglecting to appreciate and celebrating a job well done. It is of importance to share information and knowledge, all aspects leading to a flourishing organization. But in order to accomplish this, there is a need to organize the endeavor.

Although the average center usually is a small organization, the leadership environment can be very extensive and demanding. A new leader can have conflicting expectations, meet big challenges and, above all, still try to be a good leader. But what are the benefits of organizing your cultural center? According to Byrnes (2022), at least these following four points are its benefits:

1 Organizing helps to clarify who is supposed to do what
2 It establishes who is in charge of whom
3 It defines the suitable channels of communication
4 It helps to make clear where resources need to be applied to meet objectives

As a result, an arts organization such as the cultural center needs to thoroughly examine the adjustment of both the plans, budgets, processes and the people in furtherance of carrying out the mission and goals effectively (Byrnes, 2022). The organizational structure needs to be stable, but not inflexible. Both formal and informal systems can evolve inside a cultural center and the increasing effect of people and projects interacting furthers the production of a comprehensive social system addressed as an organizational culture. An organization will most likely also develop social systems based on beliefs, myths, rituals, language and shared values as conveyed by the behavior of both the employees and the leaders.

An organizational structure is not at the core of the cultural centers mission, but a useful tool to execute that very mission (Saintilan and Schreiber, 2018). It should support the objectives of the center. As anticipated, organizational structure is not something you start planning. First comes the *objectives and strategy*. Likewise, if the center is *specialized* in its productions, this has to be considered in the structure as well. If there is a need for special teams for operations, buildings, marketing and such, a thought should be given to *departmentalization*. Who does what, and which *chain of command* is applied? At some point somebody has to make a final decision. As pointed out in Section 1.1, the cultural centers seldom have many employees, but still, when it comes to the organizational structure, the amount of supervised people a manager has should be decided upon, that is the *span of control*. As to the decision-making, should the center have a *centralized or decentralized* decision-making process? A rather simple division between these would be to explain the former as an orderly decision-making model, and the latter as a more democratic one. And how *formalized* should the employee's roles be? Should there be more or less room for autonomy and discretion? The organization itself may have *organic or mechanic structures*, that is, highly formalized, structured and hierarchical or more fluid and less formalized. Arts organizations usually prefer the latter (Järvinen, 2021).

When managing performances for an audience or opening an exhibit at a particular place and point in time, it is essential to be aware that this process calls for detailed crosswise coordination between numerous working areas in a cultural center. This is due to the fact that every art form has over time evolved their processes as to best suit the work being done in getting the work that will be shared with the audience ready. This does not only concern the artistic work, it also concerns the managerial work behind (or beside) the artistic. The organizing of the cultural centers therefore has a major impact on the work to be done. Cray et al. (2007) in fact argued that arts organizations regularly run into difficulties with management owing to a divided organizational structure, *because of the need to balance aesthetic considerations with ensuring the viability of the organization* (p. 298).

This is something that also became apparent during this study, as most of the centers operate under a sort of dual leadership structure, where both the administrative and artistic side dominate. Albeit this model has some advantages, it may become problematic in the long run. Why? Simply because extensive internal tensions between administrative and artistic staff potentially leads to a halting in decision-making as well as long-term planning (de Voogt, 2006). Now, cultural centers usually do not have their own artistic staff, but do nevertheless work in close proximity with the artistic tenants. Furthermore, the case may also be that the arts manager in fact foremost advocates arts and culture, and (for instance) the financial director stands alone with the economic responsibility.

According to Hommes and de Voogt (2006), this division is due to few individuals possessing the characteristics that are needed to manage both areas. This sort of dual structure has become somewhat of the norm in arts organizations and is unavoidable simply because of the lacking experience as well as cross-training amongst the leaders. Putting it simply, most artistic leaders do not have the administrative skills that is needed to run an arts organization, and again, most administrative leaders do not have the artistic skills that is needed to advance an artistic vision.

When working with such dualistic leadership, it is not consistently evident as to what degree these two sides interact or overlap at any given level within the cultural center. The ways to communicate may be complicated, and processes such as strategic decision-making for the whole organization, as one example, suffer. This study does not aim to challenge the need to operate under such a dualistic management structure, or for that matter conceal the benefits of it. Rather, the intention is to examine whether the organizations would benefit from constructing a management structure, even if within a dual leadership model, that aims attention at and diminishes the split between artistic and managerial sides.

When organizing a cultural center, the divide may also be on a structural level. The three Finnish culture centers have consistently chosen to separate property owners and business owners. In Helsinki and Karis, foundations have been established whose sole purpose is to own and manage the respective culture centers. In Jakobstad, on the other hand, the Foundation for Åbo Akademi University owns most of the campus, but unlike the foundations in the other two culture center, it is neither poor nor owner of a single culture center. The difference between these foundations is the reason for the investment. In Helsinki and Karis, the foundations' mission is to enable activities, while the campus in Jakobstad is a pure investment object for the Foundation for Åbo Akademi University. In addition, the concert hall itself in Jakobstad, if we choose to draw the boundaries of the culture center there, is owned by YH Novia. In these pandemic times, it can be noted that it is probably Jakobstad that has coped best with the problematic situation as to absent tenants and audience. This is due to stable and versatile finances of the business maintainer YH Novia, whose finances do not rest solely on the revenues of the center. However, none of the cultural centers have survived unaffected – apart from the cultural center Fokus, obviously, as the center is not built yet. But in the future, Fokus will probably have somewhat the same situation as Kvarteret Victoria, and will thus be equally affected by crisis. The informants in Karis and Helsinki believe, after all, that the organizational form does not significantly affect their activities. On the contrary, they see advantages in the foundational form as it provides a clear division of responsibilities and a sufficient accounting obligation. Something that facilitates the follow-up and reporting of the businesses.

At the following level, beneath the property owners (the foundations), in all of the Finnish cultural centers there are the business maintainers. In Helsinki it is Teater Viirus, in Karis VNUR and in Jakobstad it is Jakobstads Konsertsal Ab. If we use the pandemic as a marker to assess sustainability in the organizational structure, we can state that the decision to differentiate between owners and operators has had its advantages – it has given the property owner respite. The business maintainers, on the other hand, have managed in different ways: Teater Viirus in Kvarteret Victoria receives state support for the theater activities and some state subsidies due to COVID-19 restrictions, but the theater still rely on ticket revenues that have now been absent. VNUR in Kulturhuset Fokus also rely on of subsidies and ticket revenues, even though in practice they have not yet had to endure the hassle of conducting business in a culture center during a crisis. Both organizations also have staff. Jakobstads Konsertsal Ab, on the other hand, has no staff of its own (apart from hourly employees who were unemployed during the pandemic), since the permanent employees are employed by YH Novia (the property owner). Jakobstads Konsertsal is a limited company, while the former, Teater Viirus and VNUR, are associations. Certainly, all three actors have other fixed costs, and the pandemic has disturbed all three of them but in different ways.

The Swedish cultural centers have not organized their centers in a similar way as their Finnish peers. Komedianten is a municipal cultural center and thus the municipality of Varberg owns both the building as well as the operations that take place within. Blivande rent their venues from the property owner (not involved in the maintenance of the cultural center activities), and they are themselves a limited company. Ifö Center has bought the factory buildings they operate in via a nonprofit limited company owned by the NGO, Sambandscentralen, that runs the cultural center. Blivande has plans to found a foundation further on, with the aim to create a platform that the volunteers would have easier to relate to – and thus be more likely to invest resources in to – than a limited company.

A common thread among half of the private centers are rather non-formalized organizational structures as well as job positions, whereas the other half has rather formalized structures and jobs. This is however not that surprising, as for instance the municipal involvement tends to have that affect, as well as in cases where many different legal organizations have to share some responsibility in the maintaining of the center. Furthermore, almost none of the centers have anything but a decentralized model when it comes to the concentration of decision-making. This was seen as prohibiting the innovative and creative work that is to be done within the center.

3.4 Taking a Step Further

When rethinking a cultural center, the point is to set an example, not merely following the trends – or other organizations. Why so? Well, following trends or simply other organizations alone leads easily to isomorphism, which means ending up as everybody else (DiMaggio & Powell, 2003) and thus lacking any advantage one could have by being slightly different. The cultural center needs thus to take a step further than merely imitating.

As stated earlier in this book, a cultural center should not focus on being what cultural centers used to have been – they need to take a further step and become what serves the arts and culture as well as their specific surrounding environment the best at any specific moment. The center needs to rethink the details of their mission statement to better be able to implement it in practice. As cultural centers do not generally produce arts themselves, it is all about the customer service they provide. Service is a very vast concept containing everything from ticket sales to assisting the event producer in practical issues in a cultural center. The question is thus not if the centers will provide services in the future – as that is their very essence of existing, it is rather what kind of service they supply to their customer. Stating the somewhat obvious: *I think that the culture centers themselves will become more and more some kind of serving functions in the future* (Informant M).

This book has furthermore taken a quite easy position as to the differences between private and public cultural centers. But as has been indicated in earlier studies, they do contrast quite a bit (Järvinen, 2021). Even if municipalities at a growing rate aim to transfer the financing responsibilities of the centers to the centers themselves, these still have the municipalities support. This may be seen as a guarantee of the continuation – which it in many ways also is. But at the same time, the pressure the private cultural centers are subjected to revenue wise can work in their advantage. They need to take that step further, taking a pause is not an option. New possibilities tend to emerge for the active ones. As one informant put it:

> *a municipal culture center that is in some way financed by municipal funds, they must only pursue culture, because that is their business mission. Everything else ends up in another category. While we have no such restrictions on us at all. We do exactly what we want.*
>
> (Informant K)

As with every organization, a gathering of individuals tends to become something more than just the sum of its parts. This is why the arts manager needs to put some mind into *how* the communication is implemented.

> *It's not just passion, it's family too. So, we create something here that very many feel as if it were their home. This is my family, these are my closest people in life. And that's why we sometimes compare this to a village.*
>
> (Informant K)

This book has frequently pointed out that arts and cultural organization function under somewhat different rules than ordinary commercial organization. While there is some truth to this, it should be emphasized that much of the ordinary work done at cultural centers do not differ from any other organization. Neither should the arts manager assume that a cultural center would not be subjected to all such trials any other organization faces. Cultural centers do not differ from any other start-up, there is an initial period where the organization is the most vulnerable and still exploring its strengths and weaknesses. Here the municipal ownership naturally makes a tremendous difference, as the risks connected to any private start-up are extensive in comparison to new public efforts.

Different bodies play an important role for most of the Nordic cultural centers. This does however not come without its own complications, as the funding bodies tend to shape for instance the evaluation processes, but also the focus of the organization. The question is, whether it is the center or the funding body that molds the future if every funding possibility (with resulting restrictions) is explored. It seems as the managers of these Nordic cultural centers are considering which subsidies to apply, in order to not deviate from their main mission.

It is not just about being adaptable (see Section 3.1). The cultural centers, just as most of organizations, need to aim at being ahead of the game. One informant emphasized their attempt to blur the boundaries of what they mean by culture in pursuance of gaining an edge.

> We see culture in a broader sense as the societal culture, which is also about how you conduct yourself with others and what ethos you have in society. And it is expressed in art as well. [...] if there is anything that makes us specific in our cultural deed, it is that we focus on sporadic art and culture. And we focus on cross-border and trans medial things. And this really has to do with the fact that we always try to encourage collaborations. And quite unexpected collaborations.
>
> (Informant K)

The maintainer of the cultural content brings the quality, entertainment and energy in to the building, and then landlords (if separate entity) can raise rents (Informant A; Informant L). The cultural center can stay ahead in the game by rethinking and always moving. To stay ahead, the next idea should already be waiting in the wings. It is imperative that cultural centers take steps to minimize the exposure to crisis in their operations. By planning ahead, the center can develop a comprehensive emergency plan that addresses crisis and emergencies of all types. Implementing strategies on how to take that step further also minimizes risks in comparison to boldly and blindly going along with every trend.

By courageously adding more innovation and creativity to the management level brings the cultural center into a fascinating dimension of intersecting ideas and experiences exploring both best practices and new business models and beyond the normal borders of your organization. As Albert Einstein supposedly stated, *we can't solve problems by using the same kind of thinking we used when we created them.* A rethinking of the approach is needed.

3.5 Case Presentation: Blivande

This case will be presented in a following manner; firstly, a brief history of the cultural center in focus. Thereafter, a quick glance on the organizational structure, the adaptiveness of the center and lastly their business model. As this center is presented in this particular section with a focus on new solutions, the idea is to introduce it accordingly.

3.5.1 A Brief History of Blivande

The cultural center Blivande is located in Frihamnen in Stockholm, Sweden, and was started in the autumn of 2018 (Blivande, 2021). Outside the house, Blivande has built an open art workshop and cultural site under the name Frihamnstorget, where everything from courses in welding, experimental performance and beekeeping takes place.

Blivande Huset and Frihamnstorget are completely participant-driven, and have their roots in the Scandinavian scene for participatory art (Blivande, 2021). Its main idea is that creative people involved in the assumptions of participatory culture are able to aid when encountering challenges in the society. Blivande maintain a 1000 m² center in the Frihamnen harbor and a 600 m² parking space full of containers.

The cultural center Blivande consists of five integrated parts (Blivande, 2021). The *Tau* (1) is a space for art, makers and community to cultivate creativity in a supportive environment, driven by a mindset of participatory culture. The space for co-working, namely *Beta* (2), is an office area. *Frihamnstorget* (3) is a container village on the parking space outside the main building, devoted to grassroots art, crafts, creativity, culture and events, and available for various initiatives. *Noden* (4) is an experiment in community building and an around-the-year place for a wide-ranging assortment of nonprofit and co-created workshops and events. Finally, *Blivande Events* (5), the venue for concerts, seminars or parties.

They particularly welcome initiatives that blur descriptions such as *artist* or *creator* (Informant K). The center aims at involving the community in decision-making as well as in new developments. In fact, the organization of Blivande has another somewhat unique characteristic, as they are attempting to build an ecosystem of individuals with separate but complementing skills and qualities, everything from dancers and painters to plumbers and software developers.

This experiment in cultivating a self-sustaining ecosystem is to develop a model that can be replicated in the future to other places around the world (Informant L). Blivande already collaborates with other communities by developing both methodologies as well as tools, and cross-referencing with each other to learn and improve together.

Blivande is Swedish for "becoming", and the core team of the center chose the name to indicate the core of what they want to cultivate, create and observe in themselves and the surrounding society (Informant K). They work under the assumption of everything – including themselves and the physical environment – being in a consistent mode of becoming. With the device of always becoming, the core team of Blivande aim to create an experimental lab for urban aesthetics, and furthermore change the forthcoming residential area by means of organically changing structures as well as co-created cultural experiences.

3.5.2 The Organizational Structure

Blivande Idéer AB is a nonprofit limited company (Trans Europe Halles, 2020). The Blivande building and Frihamnstorget are maintained as well as curated by the team of Blivande Idéer AB. The name Blivande is intended to relate both to the company as well as to the community ecosystem of artists, creators and associations active in the cultural center and in Frihamnstorget. Being a nonprofit limited company implies that shares in Blivande will not produce any income to the shareholders. Instead, the idea is that the shareholders should guide the organization according to its vision, until a foundation takes over this role in the future. As mentioned earlier in Section 3.3, the entrepreneurs have an idea of founding a foundation that further on would maintain the activities in Blivande (Informant K).

Frihamnstorget is a co-created container village in the middle of the capital of Sweden, Stockholm (Informant Q). In this container village, art, craft, creativity, culture, events and grassroots initiatives can come together in a participatory reshaping and rethinking of the city. Just as the cultural center has a participatory design, Frihamnstorget also emphasizes the concept of everybody being welcome to take part in the co-creation of the dynamic and ever-growing community, where both respect and responsibility are highlighted. The users, or the tenants of the container village, make all their decisions themselves, reshaping the parking lot to a truly communal square. Hence, Frihamnstorget has evolved to a residence for a versatile group of creative people, everything from welders and plumbers to software developers and scenographers.

The idea with the container village is to blur the limits between amateur and professional, as well as between audience and participants, in pursuance of opening up for an interdisciplinary cross-border dissemination between visitors and their members (Informant L). Under such circumstances unique alliances can take shape that in turn may lead to creative problem-solving, as in developing creative businesses using recycled materials, for instance. The Frihamnstorget container village is influenced by the cultural center's common device of *Always Becoming* (Informant K).

3.5.3 The Adaptive Cultural Center

As in many other cases, all public events came to a halt at Blivande during the COVID-19 pandemic (Informant K). Still, Frihamnstorget continued to expand. The Blivande community was never inactive during the pandemic, on the contrary. Being accustomed to a certain degree of both fluctuating structures and constant development, this uncertain situation rather enhanced the creativity and resilience of the community. As a good example of this sort of enterprising, the members of Frihamnstorget coordinated a nationwide manufacturing of 200,000 protective gowns for healthcare workers, as a response to the sudden shortage of such in April 2020. The European Economic and Social Committee awarded this initiative, called the Crisis Response, with the Civil Solidarity prize. As an example of the aforementioned self-sustaining ecosystem with the goal of replication and dispersion, visitors frequently mimic the civic engagement illustrated by the participants at Frihamnstorget. The participants are guided by the assumption that the society has a vast amount of untapped potential in accessible and dispersed civil society action, and the vision is that they can highlight this as well as inspire additional driven groups of citizens to join, not only during crisis, but in everyday life. Thus, Blivande has proven that a cultural center can evolve and renew their core mission and thereby pave the way for new solutions.

3.5.4 The Business Model

Apart from both the mission as well as the strategy to implement the mission, which has partly been presented above, the cultural center

Blivande has a few primary sources of income that make up the financial foundation for the center (Informant L). The co-working space *Beta* is the basis of the palette of incomes, generating about 30% of the turnover, and why the entrepreneurs decided to complete this part of the center first. Studio *Tau*, the space for arts and makers, generates about 25% of the revenues. *Blivande Events*, the venue for concerts, seminars or parties, also generates about 25% of the revenues. The cultural NGO *Noden* pays a rent as a long-term tenant, which makes up about 20% of the revenues.

Beside these revenues, the Blivande Idéer AB takes an overhead while carrying out different projects within the center. It is also worth mentioning, that even if the container village has a sound financial plan, the aims of this plan have not been reached yet. The entrepreneurs still trust that it will become a source of income in the near future.

As Figure 3.2 shows, Blivande too has a fairly focused and clear financial environment, even if the sources of incomes are much more focused

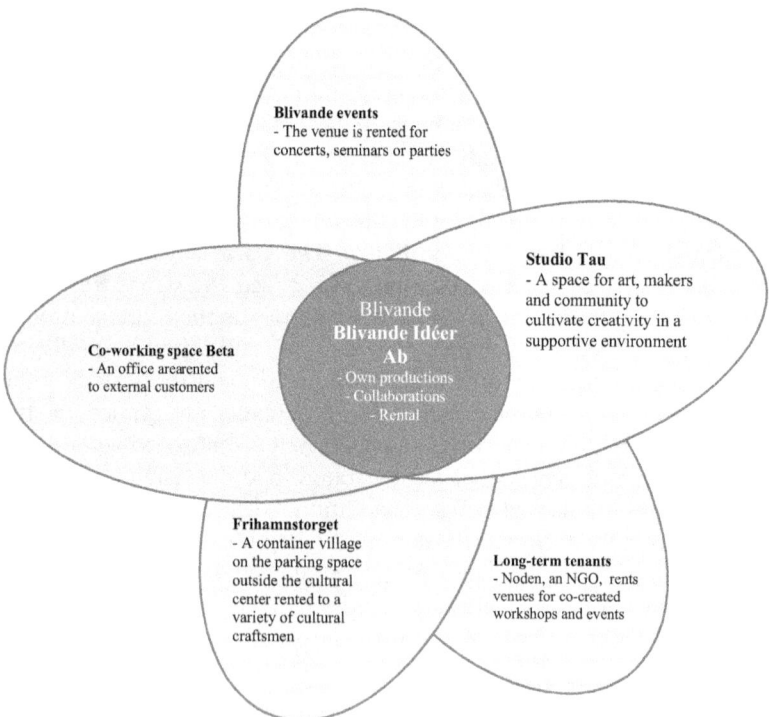

Figure 3.2 The economic environment of Blivande.

on their own activities than for instance in the case of Schaumansalen. Blivande's financial business model is also relatively evenly distributed between these five areas, as are the revenues too. In other words, there are plenty of Nordic examples of rethinking the economic environment of a traditional cultural center.

3.6 Summary and Conclusions

The centers of this study have a very different background as to how they have been established. Nevertheless, there are similarities, such as the aim to develop a hub for regional artists and cultural organizations. The results from the interviews can furthermore be extracted into the following eight points, when founding a cultural center. Note that not only the order of the points can vary, also the points themselves in that each contractor, region and culture center have its own starting point. Additionally, these steps should be revisited even after founding of the center.

1   Making of a need's analysis
2   Identifying stakeholder groups
3   Defining of the core businesses
4   Making delimitations
5   Creating a business model
6   Choosing an organizational structure
7   Developing a financial plan and
8   Building a network

This chapter has furthermore suggested that the ability to succeed in a rapidly changing world is due to the ability to foster adaptive cultures in the cultural centers. In practice, this means working intentionally with developing the organization's adaptive abilities and by continuously building new capacities that the organization can rely on when addressing the complex challenges it faces.

An adaptive cultural center will study the changes happening around it, figure out how the consumer functions within the market and then challenge old models and strategies, only to explore new ones. Such an adaptive center will evaluate what functions in a modern environment for both their markets and customers, and henceforth develop their practices and models. The thing is not to completely echo the past, nor entirely embrace the latest fad, but to do both as well as to anticipate the future.

When it comes to decision-making within cultural centers, this study shows that the cultural centers in this study use different strategies to diversify resource flows. However, since private centers can only maintain a limited level of resources, they may be forced to implement a set of limited strategies with very minimal opportunities for alternative measures. In other words, the strategic plans for the center's businesses should be ready in advance, because it is harder to implement such later on.

It is naturally also important how the cultural center is organized. This helps to clarify who is supposed to do what, who is in charge of whom and describes the suitable channels of communication. The organization of a center also highlights where resources need to be put to meet objectives. It is not unusual that arts organization run into problems due to dualistic leadership, an imbalance between aesthetic considerations and the economic viability of the organization.

It is not just about organizing or being adaptable either. The cultural centers need to aim at being ahead of the game and take the progress one step further. It is all about adapting to changes and trends in an innovative way, not imitating nor following blindly, rather being creative and anticipating the next step. Rethinking is something continuous, needed to be done every day.

In sum, the aim of this chapter was to summarize the most pressing challenges faced by leaders of the Nordic cultural centers as they chase innovation. Additionally, the chapter has offered a few insights into potential solutions discussed in the literature including examples emerging from the Nordic field. To summarize the discussion shortly, there is a need to be creative in the approaches of exploring optional directions for cultural centers.

3.7   Practical Recommendations

- When founding a new cultural center, the goal should be to consider the surrounding society and existing cultural services, the need for further services, the viability of such a project and all possible collaborators in the region.
- The objective should be that the investment for a new culture center should balance on different revenues and be at a level that makes it possible for operators to both pay rent and maintain a quality business.
- The aim is to create a platform that enables the greatest possible exchange between businesses and actors, a platform that not only

brings together a number of local tenants but acts as a glue between different levels.

• The organizational structure needs to be stable, but not inflexible. Both formal and informal systems can evolve inside a cultural center and the increasing effect of people and projects interacting furthers the production of a comprehensive social system addressed as an organizational culture.

• A cultural center should not build on earlier successes. Best practice is yesterday's shit. Organizational leaders and arts managers need a brand-new mindset and a set of tools to triumph in current circumstances. They need to rethink constantly.

Application Exercise

It's time to rethink your cultural center. What will your organization look like in the year 2030? What has happened, and in what way have you coped with the situation? The vision you create in this exercise should be one possible future. By creating alternative visions according to the framework of today, you are already in the game of rethinking your cultural center.

References

Blivande (2021). *A new world awaits.* Webpage. Accessed: 9.12.2021, available: www.blivande.com/

BOP Consulting (2018). *Business Model Innovation in Cultural Centres and Performing Arts Organisations.* Webpage. Accessed: 7.1.2022, available: http://creativelenses.eu/wpcontent/uploads/2019/02/Creative-Lenses-Survey-BOP-Consulting.pdf

Byrnes, W. (2022). *Management and the Arts* (6th ed.). New York: Routledge.

Cray, D., Inglis, L., & Freeman, S. (2007). Managing the arts: Leadership and decision making under dual rationalities. *Journal of Arts Management, Law & Society*, 36(4), pp. 295–313.

de Voogt, A. (2006). Dual leadership as a problem-solving tin arts organizations. *International Journal of Arts Management*, 9(1), pp. 17–23.

DiMaggio, P., & Powell, W. (1983). The iron cage revisited: Institutional isomorphism and collective rationality in organizational fields. *American Sociological Review*, 48(2), pp. 147–160.

Fitzgerald, S. (2008). *Managing Independent Cultural Centres. A Reference Manual.* Asef, Artfactories and Trans Europe Halles. Accessed: 14.2.2022, available at: www.artfactories.net/IMG/pdf/Managing_Independent_Cultural_Centres.pdf

Fjeldstad, Ø. D., Snow, C. C., Miles, R. E., & Lettl, C. (2012). The architecture of collaboration. *Strategic Management Journal,* 33(6), pp. 734–750.

Foster, K. J. (2010). *Thriving in an Uncertain World: Arts Presenting Change and the New Realities.* Proceedings of the Association of performing arts presenters annual conference.

Järvinen, T. (2021) *Strategic Cultural Center Management.* New York: Routledge.

Kerrigan, F. & Draeby, M. (2021). Strategic Thinking in the Arts. The Mistake of the Missing Strategy. In: *Managing the Cultural Business. Avoiding Mistakes, Finding Success.* Ed: Addis, M., & Rurale, A. New York: Routledge, pp. 78–110.

Kotter, J. (1996). *Leading Change.* Cambridge, MA: Harvard Business School Press.

Rehn, A. (2003). Quick and Dirty. In: *Avhandlingen.* Ed. Strannegård, L. Lund: Studentlitteratur, pp. 45–62.

Saintilan, P., & Schreiber, D. (2018). *Managing Organizations in the creative economy. Organizational behavior for the cultural sector.* New York; Routledge.

Scott, W. R. (2014). *Institutions and Organizations: Ideas, Interests, and Identities.* California, CA: Sage Publications.

Selznick, P. (1957). *Leadership in administration: a sociological interpretation Berkeley.* University of California Press.

Silvanto, S., Linko, M., & Cantell, T. (2008). From enlightenment to experience: cultural centers in Helsinki neighbourhoods. *International Journal of Cultural Policy*, 14(2), pp. 165–178.

Trans Europe Halles (2021). *Blivande.* Webpage. Accessed: 30.12.2021, available at: https://teh.net/member/blivande/

4   Rethinking the Incentive
What Drives a Cultural Center?

This final chapter presents an assessment of the business strengths and weaknesses and its surrounding opportunities and threats, grounded in the cases examined in this study. Adaptable management of cultural centers is founded upon reading the surrounding opportunities – a task that never ends. Without regard to how you make that reading and what decisions you make, it will determine where your organization will find itself in the future.

Naturally no one has a crystal ball, but with the help of experience, one can build a reasonably reliable vision of the future for sustainable culture centers. Therefore, it is important to listen to the society at large, to stakeholders and to those active in the centers in order to be able to draw general conclusions about the future. However, it is worth noting that the informants agree that there are no general solutions. As one informant stated: *Each house is in its own context and needs to be considered separately. There can be no one answer as to is a culture center needed or not* (Informant A). Thus, there is a constant need for rethinking whatever it is that you are to do.

This chapter will start off by presenting the added value of a cultural center, defining the core businesses, looking into future perspectives, presenting a model case before finishing with a summary and some conclusions. Thereafter, the book will be wrapped up with some general concluding words.

DOI: 10.4324/9781003253440-4

Chapter Learning Objectives

After reading this chapter, you should become acquainted to:

> - The added value of a cultural center and how to isolate it
> - Defining and refining the core businesses of your cultural center
> - Focusing on the future perspectives of your field
> - The main points of this book

4.1 Rethinking the Contributed Added Value

If you have read this book up to this point, the chances are that you already know that arts organizations bring various added value to the society. Unsurprisingly, this is also mostly the incentive for cultural centers; improving and broadening the society. In contrast to the heading if this chapter (Rethinking the Incentive), this book will not aim to change this ambition. Rather, it will focus on presenting alternative methods for achieving this goal. Moreover, in order to harness the added value, you need to isolate the effect in order to improve and maintain it, and be able to present concrete evidence to those that can help your center further. Obviously, there is not one way to do this. The added value differs, just as every cultural center differs from each other. This chapter still aims at isolating some general points an arts manager might have use of.

Cultural centers often struggle to evaluate their performance on account of the tensions as well as the gaps between artistic objectives and the means in which these are measured (Järvinen, 2021). The cultural centers themselves generally do not involve themselves in the creative work – since this belongs to the tenants. But the centers do have to measure the impact of the experience, the cultural, social and well-being value of the work they do. Although it has been stressed many times in this book that cultural centers are not a production unit when it comes to arts and culture, it has also been highlighted equally as many times that they do facilitate the aforementioned fields. Thus, it would be anything but beneficial not to count the arts and culture taking place within the cultural centers as something due to those very centers, and accordingly the evaluation of the impact of these events can be seen as a part of the centers added value. Identifying, measuring and reporting social, economic as well as environmental impact is important for the cultural centers in order to be able to enhance their position in the society and thus gain better cooperation's, subsidies and revenues.

Before examining the added value of cultural centers, it must shortly be stated that organizational value is a complex topic, even without combining it to the sector of arts and culture. In management and organizational studies, the discussion of value has for instance taken a variety of forms; scholars have focused on value architecture (Li, 2020), value chains (Porter, 1985), value proposition (Xiang and Yin, 2013), or as presented in Section 2.2 – business models, when creating and delivering value (Osterwalder and Pigneur, 2010). Values, value relations, organizational norms and practices both interacts and competes in every organization, which in turn influences the behavior of any single organization. In other words, when striving to define the general added value of cultural centers, it is of value to remember that the concept has its complications and a limited section such as this will inevitably leave some blank spots.

Holden (2006) has summarized three types of cultural values in his *value triangle*. These are *intrinsic, institutional* and *instrumental* values. They may give some pointers as to what kind of values to isolate.

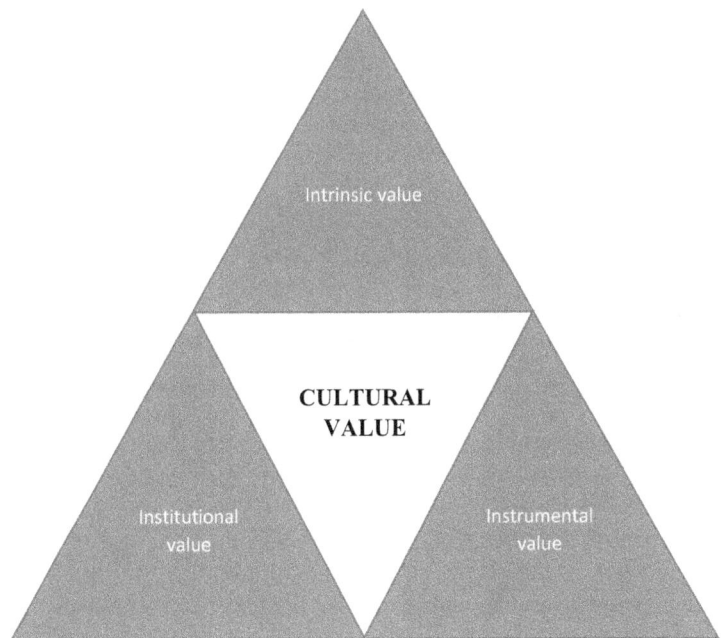

Figure 4.1 Value triangle.
Source: Adapted from Holden (2006, p. 15).

The intrinsic values are explained as a set of values relating to subjective experience in emotional, intellectual and spiritual terms (Holden, 2006). These are individual experiences that are hard to articulate generally, such as anecdotes, case studies, critical reviews, personal testimonies and qualitative assessments. They may therefore be hard to measure and standardize in order to interpret them as social phenomenas or political priorities, and the numbers they generate may not always make a persuasive case.

The institutional values in turn represent such processes and techniques that arts organizations select when trying to create value for the customers (Holden, 2006). This value can be created or destroyed when the organization engages with its customers, through both working practices as well as attitudes, and has its foundation in the mindset of public service (Calder, 2007). Cultural organizations are active creators of value and public goods, and these may be embodied in both trust and mutual respect among customers and in the context for sociability and pleasure of shared experiences and measured through feedback from the customers, stakeholders and collaborators.

The instrumental values correlate with the additional effects of arts and culture and its goal to reach a social or economic purpose (Holden, 2006). They are often demonstrated by employment rates, educational or well-being effects and represented in figures and captured in studies that report the economic and social influence of investments in arts and culture. It is naturally not easy to establish a direct causal link between the cultural offering and beneficial social or economic outcomes, which may be a result of the broad potential of culture rather than it having a specific predictable effect.

Many scholars have recognized the positive impact of arts and cultural organizations on local communities (DiMaggio and Mukhtar, 2004; LeRoux and Bernadska, 2014; Lindeborg and Lindkvist, 2013; Rushton and Landesman, 2013; Throsby, 1995; Tubadji et al., 2015). It is worth noticing that most of the scholars have been focusing on instrumental impact of the arts and cultural organization rather than a noninstrumental (Markusen, 2014), which is a result of the growing pressures for accountability that in turn leads to aiming attention at tangible products (Gori and Fissi, 2013; Liket and Maas, 2015). Furthermore, resource scarcity, competition for funding and economic recessions have compelled the arts and cultural organizations to first of all concentrate on their own economic prosperity (Weerawardena et al., 2010). Still, there is more.

One quantifiable method, thus an instrumental impact, to demonstrate how the centers contribute is by attracting new money to the region through grants from for instance the state and from national foundations (Lindeborg and Lindkvist, 2013). In addition, events at the centers attract both visitors and tourists from outside the region and are also to be considered as a model of financial stimulus, as new money from outside the region is spent by them.

Even if the economic contribution is a substantial portion of the complete value of the arts and culture as well as the community, only a piece of this contribution is easily quantifiable. As mentioned, there is the aspect on noninstrumental impact, or the intrinsic and institutional values. To name one example, the quality of life aspect that arts and cultural organizations contributes to has its own economic impacts on a region (Zembylas, 2019). Arts and culture, together with the whole bundle of local services and comforts, adds value to attracting both new residents and new businesses, may they be small or large. It is naturally difficult to determine to which degree arts or culture has an impact on the overall pull factor when attracting new residents. This is naturally also the reason to the lack of studies on this impact. However, while focusing on a broader level, both new residents and new businesses acknowledge the arts and culture along with other services, place and the general costs of doing business as decisive when choosing the location for their operations, according to many studies (Järvinen, 2021). The contributions of cultural centers are naturally much more extensive than sheer euros and cents.

In the results of the interviews a diversity of views on the added value of private culture centers can be detected. Where public spaces are completely absent, these private centers can offer a cultural platform in the region, thus an institutional value. Naturally, the informants are a rather biased party when commenting on their own added value, but at the same time they are the closest source of information we have when it comes to the practical work carried out at the culture centers – unless you consult all other actors in the house, such as customers, tenants, municipalities, organizations – but these tend to have only a limited picture of the whole, as the centers as described maintain a vast variety of activities.

The informants also emphasize the importance of the internal cooperation between the organizations and individual actors that are long-term tenants within the centers. The collaboration adds to the resources of both the cultural center as well as the organizations renting the space, and is a considerable source of ideas. At the same time, some centers point out that this collaboration could be further developed yet. Still, it adds to the institutional value of the center.

But an added value is not only about the economics. It is not about the turnover nor the profit. It is about working for arts and culture, for well-being of the customers and the development of both the customer, the artist, the society and the arts. This study present interesting viewpoints to the matter.

> *I think it's a lot about solidarity basically, I think we want to change art and how you look at art. I also think we want to change the way people interact with others. I think we want to create more opportunities for freedom, creativity and solidarity. That's a lot, because what we see around us is a society that is consistently ranked on the basis of economy. We think much more from the point of view that you help with what you can and that you get helped with what you need.*

(Informant O)

An organization may need somewhat of a competitive advantage, but as have become clear in Chapter 2, cultural centers have many levels as to the added value. Therefore, it may be beneficial to focus on the abovementioned shared and co-created value being implemented as a public good and as such as an added value, rather than merely on the competitive advantage. By definition, the public good may be the competitive advantage.

It should also be concluded that cultural centers, as representatives of arts and cultural organizations, are likely to fall under the heading of *management by values*, rather than *management by objectives* (Bilton, 2007). This can be seen as an extension of Section 2.1, as it indicates that the core values may exceed the organizational strategies and emphasize the mission focus of the cultural centers. In most cases the workers of cultural centers tend to have "noneconomic commitments to aesthetics, artistic autonomy and self-actualization, personal and social well-being, family, kinship and community and radical politics" (Banks, 2015, p. 45). But hopefully this chapter has in general isolated different means how to measure the added value of a cultural center, as well as a few examples of this happening in the focus cases. This has furthermore positively resulted in an insight that the incentive itself does not necessarily have to be rethought if it both fills a regional purpose as well show signs of viability, rather that the efficiency of capturing the value it offers in order to boost the center further should be considered.

4.2 Rethinking the Core Businesses

As may have become clear at this point of the book, there really is not one clear activity for the cultural centers to accomplish, rather they have a somewhat diffuse and a quite broad framework of possible activities to implement. The defining factors of their mission statement is customarily presented by their surrounding environment, and all the specific needs that area has, and thereby each center has a few differing but specific areas of focus. At the very core is usually the support of external artists, be they professionals or amateurs, and operating as a hub for a quantity of cultural endeavors. As has been presented earlier in this book, the cultural centers are – especially the new ones – quite agile in reacting to new trends and possibilities.

A cultural center is a diverse and multipurpose venue by its very definition. The core activities should nevertheless reflect the needs and strengths of the environment. This is especially important, as the cultural center by its very definition does not produce the arts itself, but rather supports and enables those that do so. A center should also contribute to an interaction between local actors and strive to fill any gaps in the local cultural service offering. In Jakobstad (Finland), there was already a rich music life and educational possibilities in the area, and therefore the Schauman Hall chose to focus mainly on music. In Karis (Finland), there was a need for spaces for theater activities and therefore Kulturhuset Fokus has chosen theater as its main focus area in the upcoming building. IFÖ center in Bromölla (Sweden) has clearly focused on visual artists and craftsmen.

In addition to the above mentioned examples, there is also the opportunity to fill any cultural gaps in the region with new offerings and to plan support functions around the cultural activities, for example with a restaurant or a café. In collaboration with for instance the municipality, libraries, museums and such can be placed within the center. The activities of the future private tenants should also shape the future of the culture center – a hub should rely on the strengths of its spokes. A cultural center that strives to meet the needs of citizens should also be happy to conduct a citizen dialogue with regard to future activities. Therefore, the cultural policy possibilities should be analyzed continuously.

While defining the core businesses, a rather unappreciated tool that serves well in defining the current status of the organization is the SWOT-analysis (strengths, weaknesses, opportunities, and threats). There are a quite a few differing opinions about mostly everything among the informants – a natural consequence of interviewing many people. But if the results of how the centers conduct their business today are analyzed by the means of a SWOT analysis, the following tables emerge. Due to the aim of writing a rather short book, only two analysis will be presented. We will start off with Kvarteret Victoria.

Table 4.1 SWOT analysis of the cultural center Kvarteret Victoria.

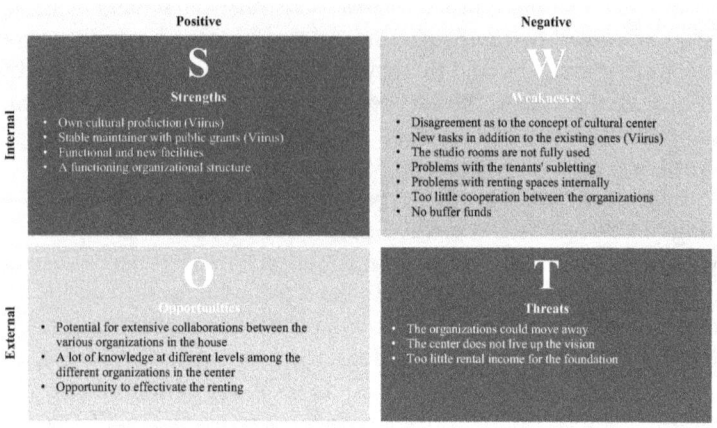

	Positive	Negative
Internal	**S** **Strengths** • Own cultural production (Viirus) • Stable maintainer with public grants (Viirus) • Functional and new facilities • A functioning organizational structure	**W** **Weaknesses** • Disagreement as to the concept of cultural center • New tasks in addition to the existing ones (Viirus) • The studio rooms are not fully used • Problems with the tenants' subletting • Problems with renting spaces internally • Too little cooperation between the organizations • No buffer funds
External	**O** **Opportunities** • Potential for extensive collaborations between the various organizations in the house • A lot of knowledge at different levels among the different organizations in the center • Opportunity to effectivate the renting	**T** **Threats** • The organizations could move away • The center does not live up the vision • Too little rental income for the foundation

(Informants A–D)

As Table 4.1 shows, there is something happening in all four sectors. In addition to the clear strengths such as a stable player as a business maintainer and functional venues, it is worth noting that most of the weaknesses are such that can be developed. The dichotomy surrounding the centers mission is (see Section 4.4) of course one of these, as are the minor problems surrounding the rental and the frugal cooperation between the long-term tenant organizations. Something that also emerges is the weak information flow among the actors in Kvarteret Victoria. It can be seen as positive that the center has many opportunities to reinforce the resources they already possess – none of the things mentioned in Table 4.1 are impossible to overcome. On the other hand, it could be pointed out that a probable consequence of not developing their resources more efficiently is that the center will not be as attractive as planned and the tenants will seek other venues to rent. It therefore also poses a threat in the SWOT table, which may affect focusing on the core businesses.

Next, we will focus on the cultural center Schaumansalen (Table 4.2). It, in capacity of the oldest of the three Finnish centers, is also the most established. It has achieved a versatile business model and has strong actors working in the background. The weaknesses are not very many, but it can be mentioned that a certain danger of the somewhat one-sided activities of their own can arise, which is due to the fact that they get government subsidies for musical concert activities and hence they

Table 4.2 SWOT analysis of the cultural center Schaumansalen.

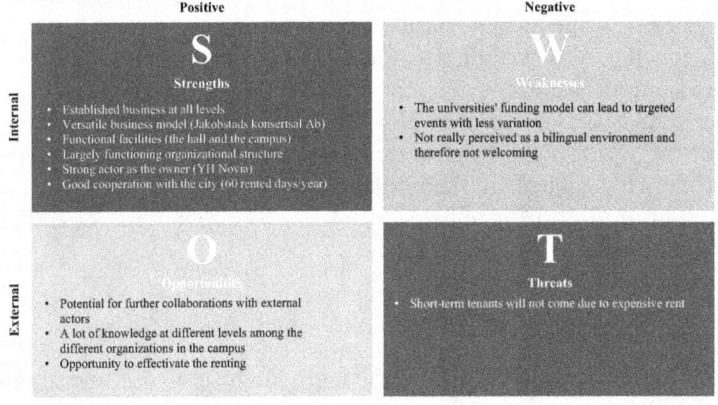

	Positive	Negative
Internal	**S** **Strengths** • Established business at all levels • Versatile business model (Jakobstads Konsertsal Ab) • Functional facilities (the hall and the campus) • Largely functioning organizational structure • Strong actor as the owner (YH Novia) • Good cooperation with the city (60 rented days/year)	**W** **Weaknesses** • The universities' funding model can lead to targeted events with less variation • Not really perceived as a bilingual environment and therefore not welcoming
External	**O** **Opportunities** • Potential for further collaborations with external actors • A lot of knowledge at different levels among the different organizations in the campus • Opportunity to effectivate the renting	**T** **Threats** • Short-term tenants will not come due to expensive rent

(Informants H–J)

have an excessive focus on concerts. In addition, the fact that people in the town seem to experience the hall as a bit too focused on Swedish (as in Finnish-Swedish) cultural content instead of Finnish. Despite the fact that they have tried different ideas in the center, they should also have many opportunities left to develop – not least in collaboration with the center's other actors. A potential threat is the absence of customers (as in short-term tenants) due to too expensive rent. Some of the informants highlighted that when pricing the venue, one could consider that a cheaper rental price often leads to more tenants, which in the long run leads to the same income as with fewer tenants at a higher price. Certainly, the wear and tear will be greater, but since cultural centers exist to implement a diversity of cultural productions, this goal is not achieved with fewer tenants.

A business model, presented in Section 2.2, is a tool for thinking and can therefore be implemented for defining and rethinking the core businesses (Baden-Fuller and Morgan, 2010). At its best, it leads to discussion about priorities and changes by focusing on opportunities as those presented in the SWOT analysis (Velu et al., 2015). When a cultural center focuses on diverse assets it may become more successful than merely focusing the cultural offering or the finances separately. The leaders of cultural centers need to be implementers of their organization's vision, be well networked, know the network, inspire staff, and build a good work community and develop expertise. The managers should be passionate about their work and want to develop it. They have the possibility to respond to the rapid changes in the environment, while keeping in mind the basic role of the centers. In doing so, they will also refine the core business of the center.

To conclude this section, a cultural center is most likely an answer to a local need. If not, the mission should be rethought. But even if the center would be an attempt to fill a void in the social and culture palette of the region, such palettes do change. The center has to be agile and follow the changes in the environment. There is no such thing as everlasting answer to a time-limited problem. The core businesses themselves need to be rethought regularly.

4.3   Future Perspectives on Rethinking the Cultural Center

While presenting some criticism and disclosure of underlying misconceptions and even flaws, this chapter on future perspectives will hopefully open up the discourse toward both positive examples as well as new approaches to managing cultural centers. The earlier chapters in this book have raised points that from hereon will be the foundation for us gazing at the future. As most of the informants have accumulated a vast amount of experience of cultural center management, this section will present ideas on how to make the culture centers more effective. Now, there are no general solutions that can be duplicated without any further thought. But naturally there are some common lessons to learn.

The whole concept of rethinking an organization is based upon a change, a change that includes letting go of old viewpoints, praxis, methods and specific activities. As Liedtka (1998, p. 123) questioned quite a while ago, … *having seen the future that we want to create, what must we keep from our past, lose from that past and create in our present, to get there?*

So how should a cultural center go about in *getting there*? Especially as the aforementioned crystal ball is not available even for the most diligent arts managers, nor for a theoretical author of a pragmatic book on such centers. Balancing between not duplicating future plans entirely from other arts organizations and recalling that change is the only constant (thus ruling out such future plans made in a specific moment immediately in the past), one can still combine the breadcrumbs left by other organizations, the combined knowledge of the staff and the constant change factor and thereby get a hunch of the future. So, let us start following the crumbs.

A natural conclusion of the interview results is as expected that the culture centers should ensure that the program content is of sufficiently high quality to attract a sufficiently large audience. The cultural centers should be places that are buzzing with life, where visitors feel welcome and where they are happy to return. The content of the activities that the culture centers offer should be based on the needs and interests of the residents and visitors, but also challenge the audience with things that they do not yet know they want to take part in. In the culture centers, everyone should have an opportunity to discover something new and grow as people.

It is quite a challenge to create a physical meeting platform that really encourages cross-border interaction between people. It happens, just as this study has to some extent shown, that this process does not succeed to meet the initial goals. The physical space of the property should still always be seen as an addition to the social space of the property, and the architectural planning is, after all, a tool for achieving the desired social function. Therefore, the actors who are to conduct the actual businesses should be given an opportunity to be heard during the construction process – if the center is founded within a new building, that is. One reason for this is the above: if the program content is not of sufficient quality, it does not attract any customers, and then in the long run there will be problems with the payment of the rent to the property owner. If the rent is too high from the beginning, the program content cannot reach the qualitative level required, and consequently the customers will not come and thus the ticket revenues will not be forthcoming either, and then there is a problem with the payment of the rent.

Through a pandemic viewpoint it can be established that the actor that rent the facilities will be dependent on subsidies if they have no other businesses or properties to balance their finances with when tenants fail to meet the rent. The rental business can sometimes carry itself, but sooner or later it may not. Those of the foundations that are wealthy and own the properties where some of the cultural centers in this study reside usually manage without subsidies, but those that lack a buffer fund, which should be the case for the majority of the cases in this study, they will be in a financial dilemma as soon as the tenants cannot afford the rent.

As has been noted earlier in this book, the level of isomorphism within the field of cultural centers has somewhat diminished, working rather in reverse now – chiefly amongst the private cultural centers. The centers seem to be very aware of their specific mission and do not want to deviate from their calling. The very first step in aiming at diverging from other organizations is not to conform to every current trend.

This applies not only to trends, but also to for instance the demands of donators and financiers.

> *the biggest challenge is probably to remember why we do this. Not to be drawn into demands or expectations from others that we really have no interest in and want to live up to. There will always be opportunities to, for example, to apply for grants for something special, but then those grants are linked to a special achievement. If it is an achievement that we are interested in living up to, then it is great to apply for those grants, then we will do it. But when it comes to subsidies that does not conform to our basic philosophy or where they try to turn us in some particular direction that we do not want to be turned in ... Then it is important that we resist and remember who we are and who we want to be.*
>
> (Informant O)

Still, it is worth noting that there is a difference between common trends and exciting prospects in line with your mission. It also seems as if these multitask centers may evolve toward something more limited. There is a need for a focus on niches. Whereas one could notice a stroke of isomorphism amongst earlier cultural center initiatives – the effect where existing organizations tend to adopt the same framework, this study could establish that isomorphism in reverse is taking place amongst new cultural centers. That is, instead of copying the mission of other centers, new centers tend to push the boundaries of the field of cultural centers by inventing new activities and ways to conduct these. Much like was the case in an earlier study concluding the very same thing happening in Finland (Järvinen, 2017). The financing models will also be challenged and changed. The informants believe that in the future we will see other types of funding models, and a greater diversity of institutions (Informant L). Still, this does not apply that everyone is going exactly in the same direction. Focusing on a niche does no more mean abandoning the multipurpose mission of the cultural centers. It only means that the center may very well have one focal point that receives more attention than the other ones. This in turn helps the managers to build up a specified network around that specific area, and helps both marketing and the attracting of customers as well.

To reinvent and rethink the intention of a cultural center does not as expected mean that the managers would have to create everything from nothing. The importance of analyzing the environment, especially actors in the same field as well as actors that are active in your center, has not diminished. But that does not mean that there are general and holistic solutions to duplicate, rather that you value what others do and try to adapt what fits in your palette. As mentioned earlier in this chapter, it is all about balancing between new solutions, existing ideas and the constant change. *I think that is the most basic thing, to value everyone else and look at how they do. Pick up their solutions, so you do not have to invent the wheel over and over again* (Informant O).

When it comes to balancing the economy, the informants believe that they are actively looking for different financing options and aiming for business activities to achieve the goals of the culture center. There is a unanimous view of this diverse resource focus as something needed to be able to offer a diverse cultural offer. As most of those interviewed state, the cultural field is not a lucrative field, but the actors can manage if they work to create a variety of sources of funding.

As Section 2.1 hopefully presented, cultural centers have a somewhat unclarified relation between arts and economics. This does not mean that both are not taken seriously, nor that the organizations are neglecting either. But having a less surplus-oriented business does not diminish the need to have a sustainable economy. Nor does it shield the center from deficits. In fact, most of the centers have experienced economic distress. Acknowledging a deficit should on the other hand not be thought as equal to cutting costs; instead, dealing with a structural deficit should be seen as rethinking the underlying business model of the center, and this could rather include examining the nature and structure of the expenses, the interplay between expenses and revenues and the connection between the fiscal measures as well as the financial strategies that support the cultural centers mission.

The interim target of any organization is – if not to create a surplus – to achieve financial sustainability in the businesses it maintains. Since the culture centers that are in focus here are quite new altogether – one is not even finished yet – there is a certain point in emphasizing something that several informants have put forward: culture centers are not a form of activity that is economically stable immediately, it takes time before they become profitable (Informant C; Informant J). You must therefore be patient and have a multi-year plan for economic sustainability.

> *You have to let it go on minus in the beginning. One cannot think that it is fast cash, but here perhaps the cultural and social value is greater than the economic. You have to see this as an investment that gives a long-term return, it will not give the owners quick repayments, but it gives so much more.*
>
> (Informant F)

It was also emphasized that the maintainer of the cultural center should focus on commercial activities as in finding an audience. The centers business operations, like other organizations, are limited by supply and demand. Albeit the cultural center's mission is generally to present a wide cultural palette of both amateurs and professionals, they have to constantly think about the financial balance, that is, how much is the audience de facto willing to pay for which event. Even though there should be a social and cultural starting point in the cultural centers, it is still often the economy that governs the assignment when the bills are to be paid. The challenge is that the cultural centers should not be too expensive to use, or else there will not be a sustainable financial balance (Informant G).

Something that has already emerged in the results is the emphasis on permanent tenants in the form of organizations that most culture centers in this study have. This leads to pure savings as the organizations share the costs. This collaboration can easily be extended to actors outside the center. A proven model is to collaborate with the city. Schaumansalen work together with the city of Jakobstad, where the city rents the hall each year, and then distributes them as support to local actors. In such a manner, the city is also involved in creating business conditions by investing in 60 evenings at the center a year, in order to then be able to offer them to regional nonprofit actors, such as choirs, associations and cultural actors who need space in the center (Informant C).

Among the culture centers that are examined here, only Schaumansalen focused solely on their own business before the company decided to act as landlord as well. In retrospect, the actors identified several problems in their earlier business model, not just the lack of profitability. As another informant puts it, there is a competitive aspect with your own customers to consider: it did prove to be quite difficult to implement in a financially sustainable way. But in addition, they did not want to compete with their own customers, that is, those who rent the center to organize events (Informant H).

The economy during the building process itself also varies somewhat between the culture centers in this study. Particularly Kvarteret Victoria demonstrated both entrepreneurship and financially sustainable solutions:

> *It was quite impressive that with a share capital of one million, [...] we managed to create this 100-million project where we then have several houses that are largely inhabited by Swedish-speakers [...]. So, this Swedish oasis has to some extent been successful and I think the organization center works very well, there are many actors and [...]*

they are mainly satisfied with the environment they are allowed to
work in, so that part has probably succeeded well.

(Informant D)

Of course, it is not fair to compare the cultural centers with each other, because naturally there are differing needs – few regions have a need for nine large housing companies in places other than Helsinki in Finland. Thus, such solutions cannot be applied to the same extent in, for example, Karis. Nevertheless, the process of building a cultural center is an important part of the future business, because the more expensive the process becomes, the higher the rents for the tenants. It is a key issue for a private culture centers success, in other words.

Surprisingly, there is a considerable absence of support functions around the cultural offer, such as restaurant and cafés. A study of Finnish cultural centers shows that this activity is by far the most common source of income (Järvinen, 2021). An informant in that study stated that their cultural center produces good food in order to be able to produce cheap culture. When asked whether there are intentions to start such activities at the centers in this study, one informant answered that it is more appropriate if an outside contractor manages that part (Informant G).

The very basis of rethinking rests on the fact that times do change. Values and opinions, even if subject for heated debates (e.g., cancel culture) and way of living at times, are not unaffected by the turning of time. Thus, cultural centers should, as stated above, should stay true to their mission but also consider how the mission positions itself in a society over time.

when I was little you would be ashamed if you did not share. But today
it is more the case that you should be ashamed if you are poor, or if
you do not have the right to rob yourself. There, I think that cultural
centers have a responsibility, just as libraries have a responsibility.
And that the rest of us have a responsibility to defend those places. It's
about civilization, maybe in the end, what kind of society do we have?
How do we want to live together?

(Informant O)

The economic reality is also that municipalities may not have the possibility to maintain a public cultural center in the future (Järvinen, 2021). This will in turn inevitably lead to a diminishing number of cultural centers or and most likely to more private initiatives. Informants in this study also confirmed this development, as for instance when laying the foundation for Ifö Center together with the municipality, until they informed the current maintainers that they *"neither wanted nor could run it"* (Informant O). Thus, a NGO was founded for the task.

Cultural centers do recognize the difficult funding landscape, and there seems to be an acceptance that things have a tendency of not standing still. Some of the centers see opportunities in this new landscape, and are thereby subsequently adapting their business models. Others seem however to move more cautiously into this new world. This may be a development of the changes introduced to their internal structures as a result to budget cuts, which have left some cultural centers struggling to keep up. The key point in this section is that whatever the incentive is to found a center, it should be carefully considered when implemented, adjusted regularly according to the vision of the management, and adjusted again according to the outcome. The future perspective is to constantly rethink the organization.

4.4 Case Presentation: Kvarteret Victoria

The cases in this book are presented in a following manner; firstly, a brief history of the cultural center in focus. Thereafter, a quick glance on their organizational structure and lastly their business model. The idea of presenting this particular center under the chapter heading of rethinking the incentive is also to apply that very lens on the presentation. What drives the cultural center Kvarteret Victoria?

4.4.1 A Brief History of Kvarteret Victoria

In the late 1990s, the City of Helsinki in Finland announced that they would build a new residential area on Busholmen (Informant C). It gave rise to an idea that, however, matured for a number of years. A private initiative led to a first meeting for a working group in 2006. This working group, consisting of three individuals, intended to book an entire block at Busholmen – something that would prove possible in 2008. The goal was to build nine housing companies of different types, by *Hitas* (housing built on plots of land owned by the City of Helsinki with a price and quality regulatory system and thus subsidized by the city (Hel. fi, 2022)), *Ara* (agency of the Finnish Ministry of the Environment in charge of construction grants and subsidies (Ara, 2022)), freely financed housing and so forth. With the help of the surplus of these housing companies the further aim was to build a cultural center in the same neighborhood. The idea was to create a Finnish-Swedish society within the framework of a neighborhood with various services on top of the cultural center, without limiting the right of residence to the language. The construction project itself had a turnover of approximately one hundred million euros and resulted in the nine above mentioned housing companies and the spaces owned by the foundation (Informant C). Today, the foundation manages a cultural center of almost 2000 m².

4.4.2 The Organizational Structure

An association was founded in 2009 to have a legal entity with the right to receive support and employ a representative (Informant C). One million euros in basic funding was received from the Tre Smeder Foundation and the association Föreningen Konstsamfundet r.f., and the site was reserved on Busholmen in Helsinki in 2010 (Informant B). At a later stage, the initiators also received support from the Standertskjöld Foundation and the Foundation for Culture and Education Investments (Informant D).

The Stiftelsen Kvarteret Victoria Sr. foundation was founded in January 2011 and acted as the constructor for the building project. When the project was completed, the constructor, that is, the share property company owned by the foundation, handed over finished houses and/ or properties to the other actors (Informant C). The real estate limited company owns a part of the main building and the foundation in turn owns the shares in that company. The foundation rents out the venues through shared ownership (Informant D).

Nowadays student housing, artist apartments, studio housing, rental housing for teachers and daycare staff, Hitas apartments and freely financed rental housing can be found at Kvarteret Victoria. For example, the foundations Stiftelsen Tre Smeder, Standertskjöldska fonden, Stiftelsen Brita Maria Renlunds Minne s.r. as well as the association Teknologföreningen own their own housing companies in the neighborhood that they have bought from Stiftelsen Kvarteret Victoria foundation, while the city of Helsinki has a daycare center, Pärlan, with room for 60 children in Kvarteret Victoria (Informant D). The Stiftelsen Kvarteret Victoria foundation kept two floors in one building, the cultural center, facing the street Medelhavsgatan. On the lower floor there are business premises for a restaurant and a shop as well as for the culture center itself, that is, the Victoria Hall, and the associated studio spaces that the theater Teater Viirus rents. There is also an amphitheater on the yard, which unfortunately has not yet been in great use so far (Informant A). On the second floor the organization center where several different Finnish-Swedish organizations rent office spaces can be found (Informant D; Informant C). At the time of writing this book, the organizations are Finlandssvenska Mathaförbundet (the Finnish Swedish Martha Association), DOT – the Association for Drama and Theater, Finlandssvenska filmcentrum (the Finnish-Swedish Film Center), Sykustens Landskapsförbund (the South Coast regional Association), SAMS – the Swedish Association for Disability, Finlandssvenskt samarbetsforum (the Finnish-Swedish Cooperation Forum), ACE-Production and Affärsmagasinet Forum (Kvarteretvictoria.fi, 2021).

4.4.3 The Business Model

The initial goal was that the sale of the other properties would generate a fairly large surplus, which would be sufficient to run a cultural center with its own production staff (Informant D). Unfortunately, the calculations were not fully met and the profit was not large enough for the foundation to take any financial risk in its future operations. They therefore began to look for a tenant who could manage the cultural activities. That tenant became, as earlier mentioned, the theater Teater Viirus.

Initially, it was thought that Teater Viirus would be one of several tenants in the cultural center, but after negotiations it was decided that Viirus would be the main tenant who then rents the hall to third parties (Informant A). The intention was further that the cultural center would be run with artistic openness where different actors share the space during the day, in the style of yoga in the morning, film screenings and children's workshops during the day and concerts and theater in the evening. However, Viirus made clear that this was an impossibility, as there is no economy for them to maintain such activities (since neither the real estate association nor the foundation were interested in maintaining the activities themselves), and it would be problematic for a theater to dismantle its décor from the stage on a daily basis in the middle of their performance period each time an outside actor needed the stage (Informant D).

The Stiftelsen Kvarteret Victoria foundation originally aimed at opening a more regular cultural center, but as the process of building and selling houses and properties in the other parts of the block did not go exactly according to plan, they no longer wanted to maintain an unsustainable economic activity – that is, a regular cultural center (Informant C). The vision was thus changed on the property owner's

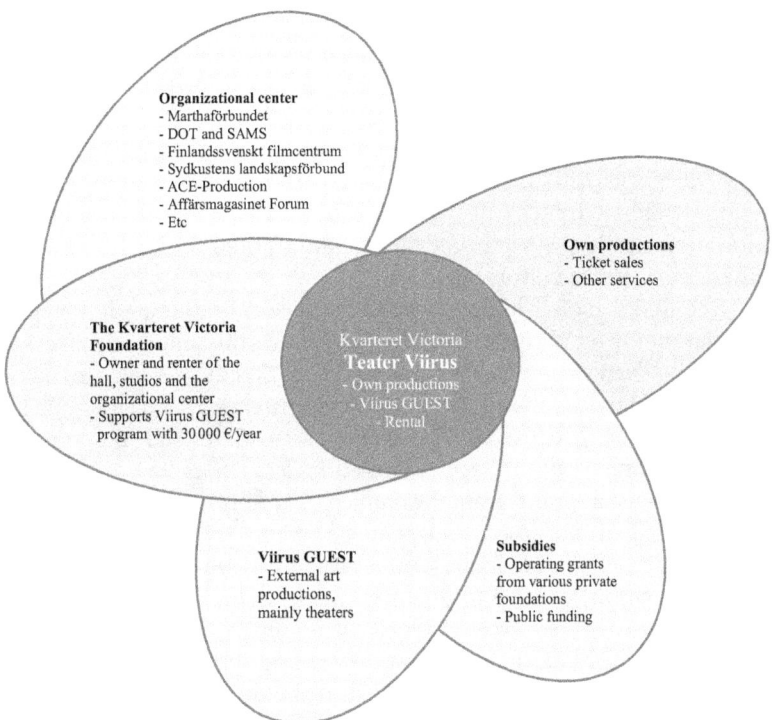

Figure 4.2 The economic environment of Kvarteret Victoria.

initiative, for Teater Viirus had no intentions to act according to the frames of a traditional cultural center (Informant A).

As can be seen from Figure 4.2, the cultural activities in this culture center are run quite a bit like a traditional theater, with ticket revenues from their own productions as well as both state and private subsidies. In addition, the theater enjoys extra support from the Stiftelsen Kvarteret Victoria Foundation in order to maintain other cultural activities by external actors (Viirus GUEST) in addition to its own operations. Unlike some of the other cultural centers in this study, the presence of the other organizations in the building does not entail any financial benefit for the maintainer of the cultural activities (Teater Viirus) – in addition to the annual support they receive from the Stiftelsen Kvarteret Victoria foundation, which can be classified as an indirect result of the rental income the foundation receives from the organization center's tenants.

The Stiftelsen Kvarteret Victoria foundation now has a CEO (approximately 20%of working hours) to ensure that things run as they should in the building (Informant B). Viirus GUEST, as the concept with outside artists at the Victoria Hall is called, started in the autumn of 2017 in Viirus's premises at Busholmen (Viirus.fi, 2022). Over 30 productions have been implemented within the framework of what Viirus calls the curated guest performance program (Viirus GUEST). The purpose is to be able to offer a diversity of art and cultural offerings in the Victoria Quarter, and to offer available spaces to other actors in the cultural field.

Even if the actualization of the initial idea of gathering a financial foundation for the cultural activities by building different housing companies and further on placing them on the market did not succeed completely as intended, the idea itself is interesting. As such, it is not an example of the incentive itself, rather a means to an end; the impetus of maintaining a cultural center was to be less dependent on external resources, such as grants from the municipality or private donators. Seen through the lenses of resource dependence theory (Pfeffer and Salancik, 1983) a parallel can be drawn to this case. The idea with the theory is that resources are the key to organizational success and the access and control over these resources is a basis of power. If controlled by actors not in the control of the organization needing them, the organization must implement carefully considered strategies in order to uphold open access to resources. As such, Kvarteret Victoria presents an alternative to succeed in this. Furthermore, by building housing companies in such a scope also presents a way to build a customer basis.

4.5 Summary and Conclusions

The informants generally believe that their cultural centers have had a positive impact on the regions that they operate in and for actors active in the centers (Informant A; Informant G; Informant O; Informant L; Informant N; Informant O). The cultural centers also have an effect that extends far beyond the boundaries of the municipality in question and the centers can thus in many ways be interpreted as interregional actors. There is a consensus that cultural centers are needed in the future as well; there is a need for meeting places, entertainment and culture, but also on platforms where actors can create culture and well-being.

On the whole, it can be stated that the centers in focus of this study work well. There is some criticism, but most people seem to agree that the pros outweigh the cons. This applies to the actors at all levels in the culture centers. It is also considered that the culture centers have a clear and pronounced added value for each region and various actors who operate within the framework of the culture centers assignments. The cultural centers therefore affect society far beyond their own walls. As the two SWOT analysis shows, there are some weaknesses but also many opportunities.

Rethinking the incentive for cultural centers to involve a more economically sustainable and efficient direction goes beyond utilizing an isolated series of actions. It converges with how a cultural center sees itself and its customers. As important that it is to redefine the depth of the cultural service the center provides, so is it to rethink and redefine the administration. This can also lead to a redefining and expansion of the concept of "customers". It may in fact require rethinking traditional approaches to mostly everything.

At this point of the book, it should be apparent that there are no general solutions for cultural centers. But it should be equally apparent that rethinking an organization's mission, vision and strategy is not about admitting that they were wrong to begin with. It is about refining them according to the changing environment. And yes, in some cases there may be a need for changing the basic premises altogether – these things do happen.

The challenge is to be (even) more customer-focused, more innovative, more agile, more sustainable, more inclusive. This is of course much easier said than done. The trick is to work on your ability to define problems and find causes, to own the problem until you find a resolution. The aim should be to identify workable solutions or to work with other resources in order to resolve the issue. The solutions should be implemented proactively and changes done in time to keep small problems from developing into big problems.

A critical part of success is to fulfil each customer's requirements. Nevertheless, to provide an outstanding customer experience, the cultural center has to surpass their expectations too. Thus, it is important to predict your customer needs by using research; analyze your customer patterns, see where your organization stands, and develop your specific business correspondently. And how is this done, you might ask? The best way is to start with existing data, data you probably already have access to. Good ways to access data is for instance to interview stakeholders, to interview customers, to map customer processes, to map the customer journey, to conduct customer and stakeholder surveys and to analyze your competition.

Cultural centers will not succeed if the aim is just to function as a showroom for the supposed existing culture and arts in the local environment. A cultural center needs to identify distinct goals and thereafter develop strategies that will help it in achieving those goals. It is important to identify promising business concepts and then break these down into manageable packages. This process involves looking closer at fields of production and products in a stepwise manner. Cultural centers should take a careful look at their existing processes and aim to boost collaboration, in addition to simplifying how the organization functions in whatever place possible.

Updating, revising as well as rethinking your cultural center may not be the easiest project, but it's a critical step in an ongoing pursuit of keeping the center viable, appealing and resilient. Naturally, the correct time for rethinking and updating is when the organization is healthy, the activities lay aligned and are advancing the centers strategic priorities. However, leaders usually become aware of a need to rethink at the point when things are not going as planned. This may be seen as the first thing to rethink – the organization needs to be revised and updated whilst everything is running smoothly, otherwise the amount of work may become insuperable. So, do not procrastinate. This is the very opposite of rethinking.

As the demands for accountability and efficiency increases, many arts and cultural organizations need to rethink their methods to enhance their capacity and their organizational effectiveness (Gori and Fissi, 2013; Liket and Maas, 2015). While becoming more receptive to changes usually brings along a competitive advantage, but naturally an exaggeration may lessen the organizations ability to pursue larger societal objectives.

How do you change the habits of developing your organization? Well, certainly not alone. Any organization prosper when the stream of information as well as ideas is both accurate and timely. An ideal leader communicates to inform, convince, coach and stimulate. The personnel share ideas, learn from one another, and keep everyone informed about opportunities, progress, problems and solutions. The thing is that effective communication, no matter if it is written or verbal, allows you to communicate your vision, to show the way forward, as well as to inspire others to work together toward a common direction.

Cultural centers need to rethink to both survive and thrive in a constantly changing competitive environment. How to stay ahead of the curve? A first step would be to make rethinking your priority. To attract all sorts of contributors and leaders at all levels to initiate innovations, whether small or large. It demands keeping an eye out for what customers need and want – this may be both new and improved experiences, products, services or solutions. In practice it means producing a great quantity of ideas and developing the best ones as they are reconstructed into something tangible. It also means continually improving managerial and operational processes – a replacement may also be required – while using the latest research as well as technology as a foundation.

Rethinking also includes reevaluating your cultural centers business model, that is, the value proposition, its markets, revenue streams and so forth. As a manager for a cultural center you have to take initiative and cooperate with individuals who see things differently. You have to be comfortable with taking risks, as well as to experiment and thereafter apply what you have learned from both mistakes and failures.

Cultural centers should have a clear focus on the core business and on the business model in order to achieve financial sustainability, a sufficiently diverse income palette and a good foundation to stand on – a building that is suitable for the purpose and where rent is affordable. The plan should be articulated and long-standing. It is important for the business maintainers to have the opportunity to make a profit while developing the business and finding customers. The long-term tenants constitute an important financial foundation in the economy. There should be a balance between quality and economy; too much focus on either can overturn the business.

4.6 Practical Recommendations

When rethinking a cultural center (or an arts organization for that matter), consider the following:

- The centers can be measured within the dimensions of intrinsic, institutional and instrumental values, in order to isolate the effect, improve and maintain the centers and be able to present concrete evidence of the added value.
- The core activities should reflect the needs and strengths of the environment.
- Arts managers need to be implementers of their organizations vision, be well networked, know the network, inspire staff and build a good work community and develop expertise.
- Focusing on a niche does not mean abandoning the multipurpose mission of the cultural centers. It only means that the center may have one focal point that receives more attention.
- Do not procrastinate – this is the very opposite of rethinking.

Application Exercise

Find a cultural center (or an arts organization within the same framework as your organization) that has either undergone considerable change or been different than the majority ever since the beginning. Try to figure out why the organization saw a need to rethink their situation, and how they went along with the change – and how they have maintained that mindset thereafter. What actions did the management take and what results did these decisions have?

References

Ara (2022). *Funding to improve housing conditions.* Webpage. Accessed: 26.3.2022, available at: www.ara.fi/fi-FI/Lainat_ja_avustukset

Baden-Fuller, C., & Haefliger, S. (2013). Business models and technological innovation. *Long Range Planning,* 46(6), pp. 419–426.

Baden-Fuller, C., & Morgan, M. (2010). Business models as models. *Long Range Planning* 43, pp. 156–171.

Banks, M. (2015). The Value of Cultural Industries. In: *The Routledge Companion to the Cultural Industries.* Eds.: Oakley, K., & O'Connor, J. Routledge: London.

Bilton, C. (2007). *Management and Creativity: From Creative Industries to Creative Management.* Malden, MA: Blackwell Publishing, pp. 51–60.

Calder, W. B. (2007). The VVM strategy for institutional success. *The College Quarterly,* 10(3), pp. 1–7.

DiMaggio, P., & Mukhtar, T. (2004). Arts participation as cultural capital in the United States, 1982–2002: Signs of decline? *Poetics,* 32, pp. 169–194.

Gori, E., & Fissi, S. (2013). From cash to accrual accounting: A model to evaluate the performance of public museums. *Review of International Comparative Management,* 14, pp. 519–541.

Hel.fi (2022). *Mitä Hitas on?* PDF. Accessed: 26.3.2022, available at: www.hel.fi/static/kv/asunto-osasto/hitas-tietopaketti.pdf

Holden, J. (2006). *Cultural Value and the Crisis of Legitimacy: Why Culture Needs a Democratic Mandate.* London: Demos.

Järvinen, T. (2017). From One Mission Statement to Two Organizational Fields: The Effects of Reverse Isomorphism in Private Cultural Centers. In: *Making Sense of Arts Management. Research, Cases and Practices.* Eds.: Johansson, T., & Luonila, M. Sibelius Academy Publications. Helsinki: Unigrafia, pp. 128–132.

Järvinen, T. (2021). *Strategic Cultural Center Management.* New York: Routledge.

Kvarteretvictoria.fi (2021). Organisationer. Webpage. Accessed: 26.10.2021, available at: www.kvarteretvictoria.fi/organisationer

LeRoux, K., & Bernadska, A. (2014). Impact of the arts on individual contributions to US civil society. *Journal of Civil Society*, 10, pp. 144–164.

Li, F. (2020). The digital transformation of business models in the creative industries: A holistic framework and emerging trends. *Technovation*, 92–93, pp. 92–93.

Liedtka, J. (1998). Linking strategic thinking with strategic planning. *Strategy and Leadership,* 10(1), pp. 120–129.

Liket, K. C., & Maas, K. (2015). Nonprofit organizational effectiveness: Analysis of best practices. *Nonprofit and Voluntary Sector Quarterly*, 44, pp. 268–296.

Lindeborg, L., & Lindkvist, L. (2013). *The Value of Arts and Culture for Regional Development. A Scandinavian Perspective.* New York: Routledge.

Markusen, A. (2014). *Creative cities: A 10-year research agenda. Journal of Urban Affairs,* 36, pp. 567–589.

Osterwalder, A., & Pigneur, Y. (2010). *Business Model Generation: A Handbook for Visionaries, Game Changers and Challengers.* New York: John Wiley & Sons.

Pfeffer, J., & Salancik, G. R. (1983). *The External Control of Organizations: A Resource Dependence Perspective.* New York, NY, Harper and Row.

Porter, M. E. (1985). *Competitive Advantage.* New York: Free Press.

Rushton, M., & Landesman, R. (2013). *Creative Communities: Art Works in Economic Development.* Washington, DC: Brookings Institution Press.

Throsby, D. (1995). Culture, economics and sustainability. *Journal of Cultural Economics,* 19, pp. 199–206.

Tubadji, A., Osoba, B. J., & Nijkamp, P. (2015). Culture-based development in the USA: Culture as a factor for economic welfare and social well-being at a county level. *Journal of Cultural Economics*, 39, pp. 277–303.

Velu, C., Smart, A., & Philips, M. (2015). *The Imperative for Business Model Innovation.* NEMODE White Paper. Cambridge: Institute for Manufacturing.

Viirus.fi (2022). *Om Viirus.* Webpage. Accessed: 31.3.2022, available at: www.viirus.fi/teater/om-teatern

Weerawardena, J., McDonald, R. E., & Mort, G. S. (2010). Sustainability of nonprofit organizations: An empirical investigation. *Journal of World Business,* 45, pp. 346–356.

Xiang, G., & Yin, Y. P. (2013). *Decomposition, Classification, and Evaluation of Business Models. The Case of Chinese Retailing.* Hatfield, UK: Hertfordshire Business School Working Papers.

5   Concluding Words

Next to its limited theoretical and mainly practical approaches, this book hopefully contains both helpful and necessary definitions of basic terms, which you as the reader may have noticed can have different meanings when used in certain regions and contexts. This idea alone steered the writing of this book, as the field of cultural centers is in many ways underresearched. And obviously, if you have come this far – I thank you for reading this book.

This book contributes to the decision-making in cultural centers about new business directions and feasible success factors in order to reach new growth opportunities. It also emphasizes the avoiding of duplicating the work approaches of other organizations and gives priority to the opportunities to practice your own style when steering your center toward the future. There is no longer a need for a straight off imitation. Rather, set the stage according to current needs, examine the alternative solutions that most probably can be found within the field, choose the most suitable and build your own specific model.

Anticipating your customer's needs shows that your cultural center sees them as your partners, that you are investing time on their behalf by thinking ahead of them. Things they had not even maybe thought of. This allows you to create an even bigger experience. But of course, good service and making the customers feel valued can only take you so far. You have to have good products and a fair price as well.

There are many limitations to the book. It is therefore important to emphasize that the cases in this book represent a very small sample of the total amount of cultural centers in the world. Each and every cultural center – wherever they may be located – represent a practical solution for the specific area they are established in, the needs and the potentiality that can be found there. There are no general solutions the can be applied everywhere. The aim with this book has solely been to raise awareness of the need to rethink the purpose of cultural centers – are we

DOI: 10.4324/9781003253440-5

doing what we are supposed to be doing and are we doing it efficiently? I hope this book raised some questions and maybe it also helped you along the way to find some answers to these questions – answers that apply to your specific cultural center. And would you like to read more about cultural centers, you can always take a look at the book *Strategic Cultural Center Management*.

So, do not restrain yourselves to old mission statements or general assumptions, do not be limited to the way things have used to be or old successes; rather analyze your environment, assess your capabilities – reconsider, redefine and rethink your cultural center!

About the Author

Tomas Järvinen is CEO of Folkhälsan Education, Finland. He has recently (2021) published the book *Strategic Cultural Center Management*, published by Routledge, as well as the book *Svenska kulturhus i Finland–hur, var och varför?* (*Swedish Cultural Centers in Finland – How, Where and Why?*), published by Svenska kulturfonden. Järvinen is also a musician and has won two Emma (Finnish Grammys) awards (2018 and 2020) for best children's music in Finland, and is nominated again in 2022. He holds a PhD in Arts Management (Sibelius Academy, University of the Arts, Helsinki).

Index

For Product Safety Concerns and Information please contact our EU
representative GPSR@taylorandfrancis.com
Taylor & Francis Verlag GmbH, Kaufingerstraße 24, 80331 München, Germany

www.ingramcontent.com/pod-product-compliance
Lightning Source LLC
Chambersburg PA
CBHW072211170526
45158CB00002BA/548